A WORLD AT
MILITARY HISTORY
1861-1945

A WORLD ATLAS

by ARTHUR BANKS

OF MILITARY HISTORY

1861-1945

DA CAPO PRESS

Library of Congress Cataloging in Publication Data

Banks, Arthur.
  A world atlas of military history, 1861-1945.

  (A Da Capo paperback)
  Reprint. Originally pub.: London: Seely Service,
1978.
  1. Geography, Historical—Maps. 2. Military
history—Maps. I. Title.
G1030.B272 1988   911   88-675220
ISBN 0-306-80332-1 (pbk.)

This Da Capo Press paperback edition of *A World Atlas of Military
History 1861–1945* is an unabridged republication of the edition
published in London in 1978. It is reprinted by arrangement with
William Heinemann Ltd.

Published by Da Capo Press
A Member of the Perseus Books Group
http://www.dacapopress.com

13 12 11 10 9 8 7 6

CONTENTS

III Strife and Alignments

IV The First World War

V **The Inter-War Years**

VI **The Second World War**

ACKNOWLEDGEMENTS

During the preparation of this atlas, I was aided by a number of friends and military organizations. I wish to express my gratitude and thanks to Mrs J Campbell, Mr R Holmes, Mr E Jennings, Mr A Palmer and Mr M Willis. In particular, the Imperial War Museum and the Royal United Services Institute for Defence Studies were generous in the facilities they placed at my disposal. I am also indebted to Messrs Heinemann Educational Ltd for allowing me to reproduce twelve maps which I originally drew for my *Military Atlas of the First World War*.

Arthur Banks

I

PHYSICAL FEATURES

EUROPE: PHYSICAL FEATURES

This generalised map is included so that local campaigns can be seen in relation to geography.

KEY

Low land (0-3000 feet).

Intermediate land (3000-6000 feet).

High land (over 6000 feet).

0   500
Miles

© Arthur Banks 1975

URAL MOUNTAINS

Caspian Sea

Volga

Don

Dnieper

L.Onega

L.Ladoga

Dniester

CAUCASUS MTS

PONTIC RANGE

TAURUS RANGE

Black Sea

CARPATHIAN MTS

TRANSYLVANIAN ALPS

BALKAN MTS

PINDUS MTS

DINARIC ALPS

SCANDINAVIAN HIGHLANDS

Baltic Sea

Vistula

Oder

Elbe

Rhine

Seine

Danube

Sava

A L P S

Po

APENNINES

Rhône

Ebro

Mediterranean Sea

North Sea

Bay of Biscay

ATLANTIC OCEAN

CANTABRIANS

PYRENEES

CENTRAL SIERRAS

SIERRA MORENA

S. NEVADA

Tagus

ASIA : PHYSICAL FEATURES

3

KEY

☐ Low land (0-3000 feet).

▨ Intermediate land (3000-6000 feet).

■ High land (over 6000 feet).

This generalised map is included in order that local campaigns can be seen in relation to geography.

© Arthur Banks 1975

1000 Miles
0

PACIFIC OCEAN

ARCTIC OCEAN

EUROPE

AFRICA

INDIAN OCEAN

SOUTH CHINA SEA

BAY OF BENGAL

ARABIAN SEA

MEDITERRANEAN SEA

RED SEA

BLACK SEA

CASPIAN SEA

ARAL SEA

L. Balkash

L. Baikal

URAL MTS.

KUNLUN MTS.

HIMALAYAS

MT. EVEREST

Hindu Kush

Indigirka
Lena
Yenisei
Ob
Irtysh
Tobol
Ural
Volga
Don
Dnieper
Dniester
Tigris
Euphrates
Indus
Ganges
Narbada
Godavari
Krishna
Irrawaddy
Salween
Mekong
Sikiang
Red
Yangtze
Hwang Ho
Amur
Liao Ho

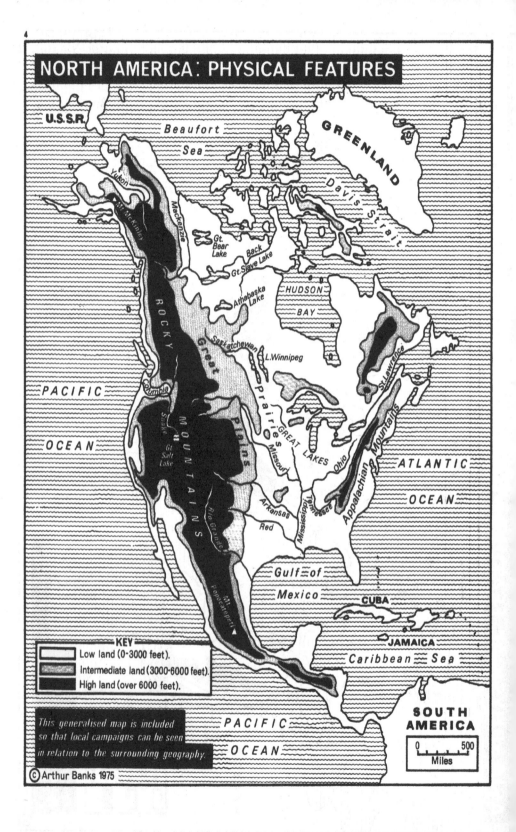

NORTH AMERICA: PHYSICAL FEATURES

4

U.S.S.R.

Beaufort
Sea

GREENLAND

Davis Strait

Yukon

Mt. McKinley

Mackenzie

Gt.
Bear
Lake

Back

Gt. Slave Lake

Athabaska
Lake

HUDSON

BAY

ROCKY

Saskatchewan

L. Winnipeg

St. Lawrence

PACIFIC

Columbia

Great Plains

Prairies

GREAT
LAKES

OCEAN

Snake

MOUNTAINS

Gt.
Salt
Lake

Missouri

Ohio

Appalachian Mountains

ATLANTIC

OCEAN

Rio Grande

Arkansas

Red

Mississippi

Tennessee

Gulf of
Mexico

CUBA

KEY

Low land (0-3000 feet).

Intermediate land (3000-6000 feet).

High land (over 6000 feet).

Mt. Popocatepetl

JAMAICA

Caribbean Sea

SOUTH
AMERICA

This generalised map is included
so that local campaigns can be seen
in relation to the surrounding geography.

PACIFIC

OCEAN

© Arthur Banks 1975

0   500
Miles

5

SOUTH AMERICA : PHYSICAL FEATURES

Caribbean

Sea

ATLANTIC

OCEAN

LLANOS

Orinoco

GUIANA

HIGHLANDS

S
Japura

Putumayo

Negro

Branco

Amazon

CHIMBORAZO

Jurua

Purus

S
E
L
V
A
S

Madeira

Tapajoz

Araguaia

Tocantins

C A A T I N G A S

Sao
Francisco

A
N
D
E
S

SAJAMA

PACIFIC

OCEAN

Pilcomayo

CHACO

GRAN

Paraguay

Parana

OJOS DEL
SALADO

ACONCAGUA

P A M P A S

Parana

Uruguay

Parana

R

ATLANTIC

OCEAN

This generalised map is
included so that individual
campaigns can be seen in broad
relation to local geography.

0	500

Miles

Arthur Banks 1975

KEY

Low land (0-3000 feet).

Intermediate land (3000-6000 feet).

High land (over 6000 feet).

▲ Important heights.

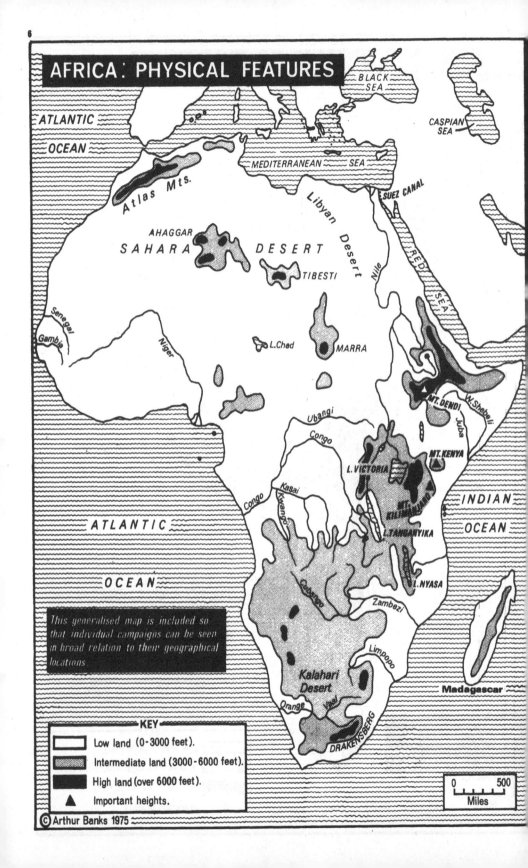

AFRICA: PHYSICAL FEATURES

BLACK SEA

CASPIAN SEA

ATLANTIC OCEAN

MEDITERRANEAN SEA

SUEZ CANAL

Atlas Mts.

Libyan Desert

AHAGGAR

SAHARA DESERT

TIBESTI

Nile

RED SEA

Senegal

Gambie

Niger

L.Chad

MARRA

Ubangi

Congo

MT. DENDI

W.Shebeli

Juba

Congo

Kasai

Kwango

L.VICTORIA

MT.KENYA

ATLANTIC

MT. KILIMANJARO

INDIAN OCEAN

L.TANGANYIKA

OCEAN

L.NYASA

Okavango

Zambezi

Limpopo

This generalised map is included so that individual campaigns can be seen in broad relation to their geographical locations.

Madagascar

Kalahari Desert

Orange

Vaal

DRAKENSBERG

KEY

	Low land (0-3000 feet).
	Intermediate land (3000-6000 feet).
	High land (over 6000 feet).
▲	Important heights.

0   500
Miles

© Arthur Banks 1975

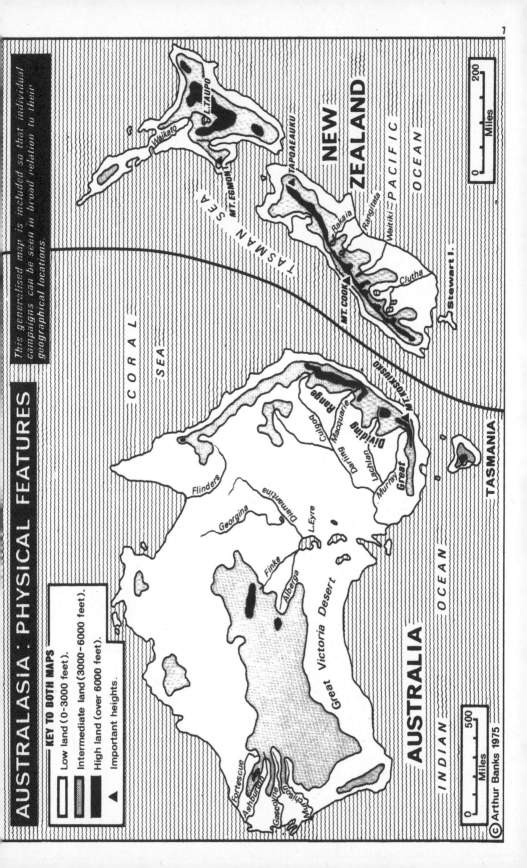

II
THE AMERICAN CIVIL WAR

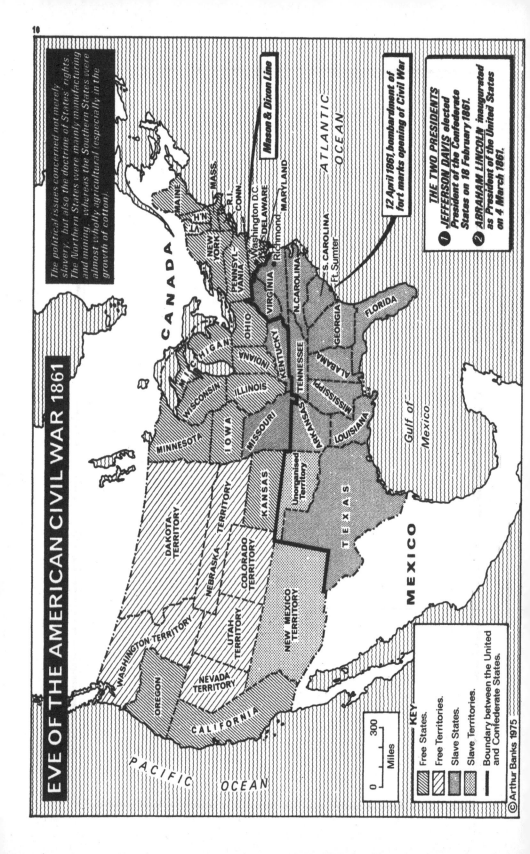

EVE OF THE AMERICAN CIVIL WAR 1861

The political issues concerned not merely slavery, but also the doctrine of States rights. The Northern States were mainly manufacturing and mining, whereas the Southern States were almost wholly agricultural (especially in the growth of cotton).

Mason & Dixon Line

12 April 1861, bombardment of fort marks opening of Civil War.

THE TWO PRESIDENTS

① JEFFERSON DAVIS elected President of the Confederate States on 18 February 1861.

② ABRAHAM LINCOLN inaugurated as President of the United States on 4 March 1861.

ATLANTIC OCEAN

CANADA

MASS.
MAINE
N.H.
R.I.
CONN.
NEW YORK
VERMONT
PENNSYL-VANIA
Washington D.C.
DELAWARE
MARYLAND
VIRGINIA
Richmond
N.CAROLINA
S.CAROLINA
Ft. Sumter
GEORGIA
FLORIDA
ALABAMA
MISSISSIPPI
TENNESSEE
KENTUCKY
OHIO
INDIANA
MICHIGAN
WISCONSIN
ILLINOIS
IOWA
MINNESOTA
MISSOURI
ARKANSAS
LOUISIANA

Gulf of Mexico

DAKOTA TERRITORY
NEBRASKA TERRITORY
KANSAS
Unorganised Territory
COLORADO TERRITORY
WASHINGTON TERRITORY
UTAH TERRITORY
NEVADA TERRITORY
NEW MEXICO TERRITORY
TEXAS
OREGON
CALIFORNIA

MEXICO

PACIFIC OCEAN

KEY

▨	Free States.
▧	Free Territories.
▤	Slave States.
▦	Slave Territories.
—	Boundary between the United and Confederate States.

0   300
Miles

© Arthur Banks 1975

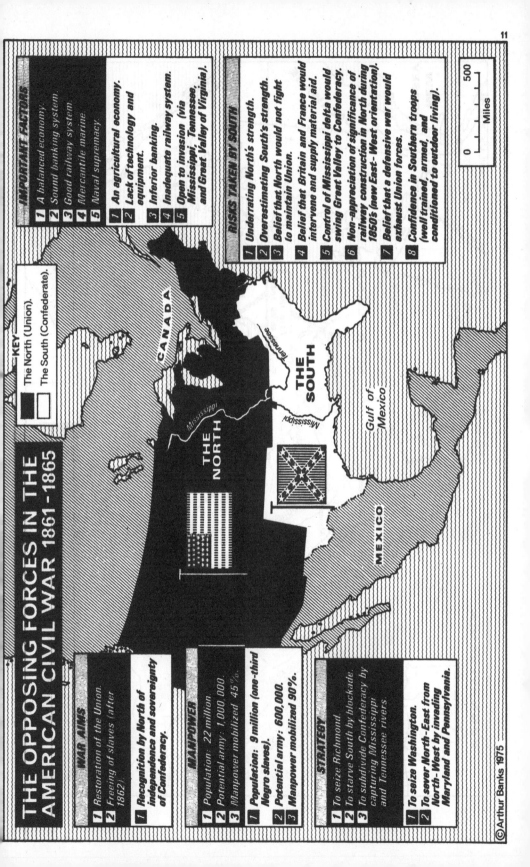

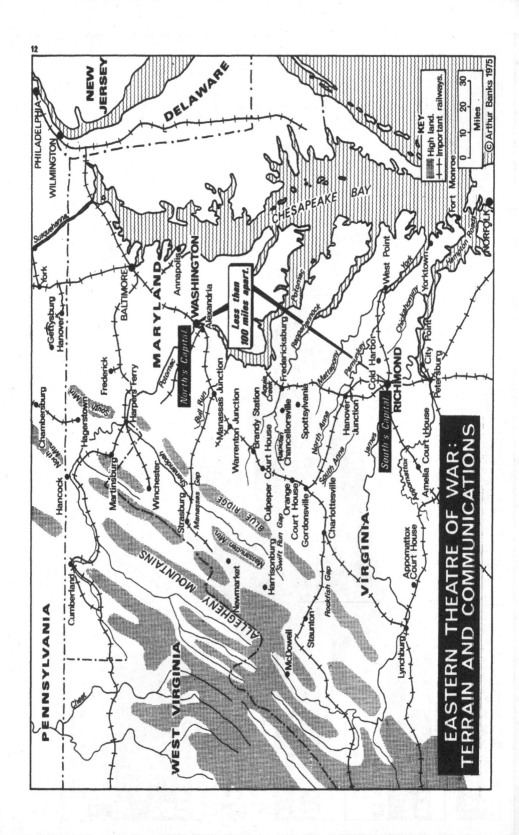

12

KEY
High land.
Important railways.
Miles
0 10 20 30

© Arthur Banks 1975

NEW JERSEY
DELAWARE
PHILADELPHIA
WILMINGTON
Susquehanna
York
CHESAPEAKE BAY
PENNSYLVANIA
Gettysburg
Hanover
BALTIMORE
MARYLAND
Annapolis
North's Capital
WASHINGTON
Alexandria
Potomac
Less than 100 miles apart.
Chambersburg
North Mtn.
Hancock
Hagerstown
Harper's Ferry
Frederick
Martinsburg
Winchester
Opequon
Cumberland
Strasburg
Manassas Gap
Massanutton Mtn.
BLUE RIDGE
Manassas Junction
Bull Run
Warrenton Junction
Brandy Station
Aquia Creek
Fredericksburg
Rappahannock
Potomac
WEST VIRGINIA
ALLEGHENY MOUNTAINS
Cheat
Newmarket
Harrisonburg
Swift Run Gap
McDowell
Staunton
Culpeper Court House
Orange Court House
Rapidan
Chancellorsville
Spottsylvania
Gordonsville
Charlottesville
North Anna
South Anna
Mattapony
Pamunkey
Hanover Junction
Cold Harbor
Chickahominy
West Point
York
RICHMOND
South's Capital
James
City Point
Petersburg
Yorktown
Hampton Roads
Fort Monroe
NORFOLK
Rockfish Gap
VIRGINIA
Lynchburg
Appomattox
Appomattox Court House
Amelia Court House

EASTERN THEATRE OF WAR:
TERRAIN AND COMMUNICATIONS

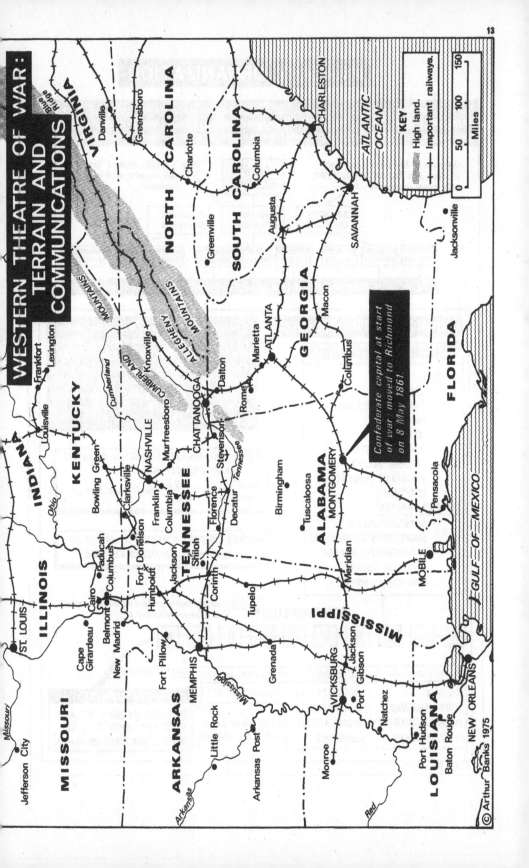

13

WESTERN THEATRE OF WAR: TERRAIN AND COMMUNICATIONS

KEY

High land.
+++ Important railways.

Miles
0   50   100   150

Confederate capital at start of war: moved to Richmond on 8 May 1861

VIRGINIA

NORTH CAROLINA

SOUTH CAROLINA

GEORGIA

FLORIDA

ALABAMA

MISSISSIPPI

TENNESSEE

KENTUCKY

INDIANA

ILLINOIS

MISSOURI

ARKANSAS

LOUISIANA

Blue Ridge

ALLEGHENY MOUNTAINS

CUMBERLAND MOUNTAINS

ATLANTIC OCEAN

GULF OF MEXICO

Danville
Greensboro
Charlotte
Columbia
Charleston
Augusta
Savannah
Jacksonville
Greenville
Knoxville
Lexington
Frankfort
Louisville
Bowling Green
Clarksville
Nashville
Murfreesboro
Franklin
Columbia
Florence
Decatur
Stevenson
Dalton
Rome
Marietta
ATLANTA
Macon
Columbus
MONTGOMERY
Pensacola
Birmingham
Tuscaloosa
Meridian
MOBILE
Jackson
Humboldt
Corinth
Tupelo
Shiloh
Fort Donelson
Paducah
Columbus
Cairo
Belmont
Cape Girardeau
New Madrid
Fort Pillow
MEMPHIS
Grenada
Jackson
VICKSBURG
Port Gibson
Natchez
Port Hudson
Baton Rouge
NEW ORLEANS
Monroe
Arkansas Post
Little Rock
Jefferson City
ST. LOUIS
CHATTANOOGA
Marietta

Cumberland
Tennessee
Ohio
Mississippi
Missouri
Arkansas
Red

© Arthur Banks 1975

MILITARY ORGANIZATION

Both sides commenced with similar organizations but changes occurred as the war progressed. Neither side started with army corps, but, in March 1862, the Union (on Lincoln's initiative) formed several of these. Strengths of units varied considerably: commanders were given maximum and minimum figures to work to most of the time.

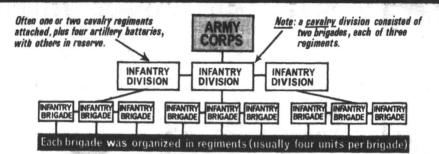

Often one or two cavalry regiments attached, plus four artillery batteries, with others in reserve.

ARMY CORPS

Note: a cavalry division consisted of two brigades, each of three regiments.

INFANTRY DIVISION — INFANTRY DIVISION — INFANTRY DIVISION

INFANTRY BRIGADE · INFANTRY BRIGADE · INFANTRY BRIGADE · INFANTRY BRIGADE · INFANTRY BRIGADE · INFANTRY BRIGADE · INFANTRY BRIGADE · INFANTRY BRIGADE · INFANTRY BRIGADE

Each brigade was organized in regiments (usually four units per brigade)

UNION INFANTRY REGIMENT

The regiment was the basic tactical unit of the United States army both in peace and war, and was similar to the British battalion. Its field strength averaged about 900 officers and men. In theory, Union and Confederate regiments were organized on similar lines but, in practice, there were many variations on the Confederate side, for example, the 55th Alabama had battalions.

REGIMENTAL HEADQUARTERS

OFFICERS:

COLONEL
LIEUTENANT-COLONEL
MAJOR
ADJUTANT
QUARTERMASTER
SURGEON-MAJOR
ASSISTANT SURGEONS (2)
CHAPLAIN

ENLISTED PERSONNEL:

SERGEANT-MAJOR
QUARTERMASTER-SERGEANT
COMMISSARY-SERGEANT
PRINCIPAL MUSICIANS (2)
HOSPITAL STEWARD

AVERAGE REGIMENTAL STRENGTHS AT BATTLE OF CHANCELLORSVILLE WERE:

UNION ———— 433 } Officers & men per regt.
CONFEDERATE — 409 }

AVERAGE COMPANY STRENGTH AT BATTLE OF GETTYSBURG WAS 32 OFFICERS AND MEN.

COMPANIES (10) Note: except heavy artillery regiments retained as infantry which had 12.

A B C D E F G H I K L

Note: 'J' omitted

Maximum strength: 101	**COMPANY**	Minimum strength : 83

CAPTAIN · SERGEANTS (4) · PRIVATES (64-82)
FIRST LIEUTENANT · CORPORALS (8)
SECOND LIEUTENANT · MUSICIANS (2) · Usually six squadrons, each of two companies.
FIRST SERGEANT · WAGGONER

CAVALRY REGIMENT

THIS HAD **12** COMPANIES AND THESE WENT FROM 'A' TO 'M' (WITH 'J' OMITTED). 725 all ranks.

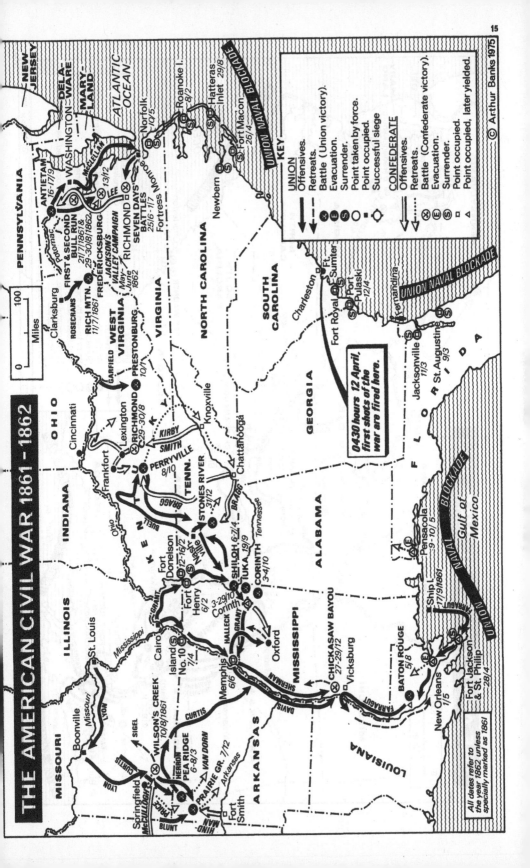

THE AMERICAN CIVIL WAR 1861–1862

© Arthur Banks 1975

KEY

UNION
- Offensives.
- Retreats.
- ⊗ Battle (Union victory).
- Ɛ Evacuation.
- S Surrender.
- ○ Point taken by force.
- ◆ Point occupied.
- ◇ Successful siege.

CONFEDERATE
- Offensives.
- Retreats.
- ⊗ Battle (Confederate victory).
- Ɛ Evacuation.
- □ Point occupied.
- △ Point occupied, later yielded.

Miles 0 100

0430 hours 12 April, first shots of the war are fired here.

All dates refer to the year 1862 unless specially marked as 1861

NEW JERSEY
DELAWARE
MARYLAND
ATLANTIC OCEAN
PENNSYLVANIA
WASHINGTON
McCLELLAN
ANTIETAM 16-17/9
Potomac
FIRST & SECOND BULL RUN 21/7/1861 & 29-30/8/1862
LEE 13/2
Norfolk 10/5
Roanoke I. 8/2
Hatteras Inlet 29/8
Fort Macon 26/4
UNION NAVAL BLOCKADE
Clarksburg
RICH MTN. 11/7/1861
ROSECRANS
WEST VIRGINIA
GARFIELD
PRESTONBURG 10/1
FREDERICKSBURG
JACKSON'S VALLEY CAMPAIGN May–June 1862
RICHMOND
SEVEN DAYS' BATTLES 25/6-1/7
Fortress Monroe
VIRGINIA
NORTH CAROLINA
Newbern
SOUTH CAROLINA
Charleston
Ft. Sumter
Fort Royal 7/11
Port Pulaski 12/4
Fernandina
UNION NAVAL BLOCKADE
GEORGIA
Jacksonville 11/3
St. Augustine 9/3
F L O R I D A
Gulf of Mexico
NAVAL BLOCKADE
UNION
OHIO
Cincinnati
Lexington
RICHMOND 29-30/8
Frankfort
KIRBY SMITH
PERRYVILLE 8/10
Knoxville
Chattanooga
KENTUCKY
BRAGG
BUELL
STONES RIVER 31/12
BRAGG
TENN.
INDIANA
Ohio
Nashville
SHILOH 6-7/4
IUKA 19/9
CORINTH 3-4/10
Tennessee
Fort Donelson 12-16/2
Fort Henry 6/2
Corinth 3-29/10
GRANT
HALLECK
Oxford
ALABAMA
Pensacola 9-10/5
Ship I. 17/9/1861
FARRAGUT
ILLINOIS
St. Louis
Mississippi
Cairo
Island No.10 7/4
Memphis 6/6
GRANT
DAVIS
CHICKASAW BAYOU 27-29/12
Vicksburg
SHERMAN
MISSISSIPPI
BATON ROUGE 5/8
FARRAGUT
New Orleans 1/5
Fort Jackson & St. Philip 28/4
MISSOURI
Boonville
Missouri
LYON
SIGEL
WILSON'S CREEK 10/8/1861
CURTIS
Springfield
McCULLOCH
PRICE
HERRON
PEA RIDGE 6-8/3
VAN DORN
PRAIRIE GR. 7/12
Arkansas
HINDMAN
BLUNT
ARKANSAS
Fort Smith
LOUISIANA

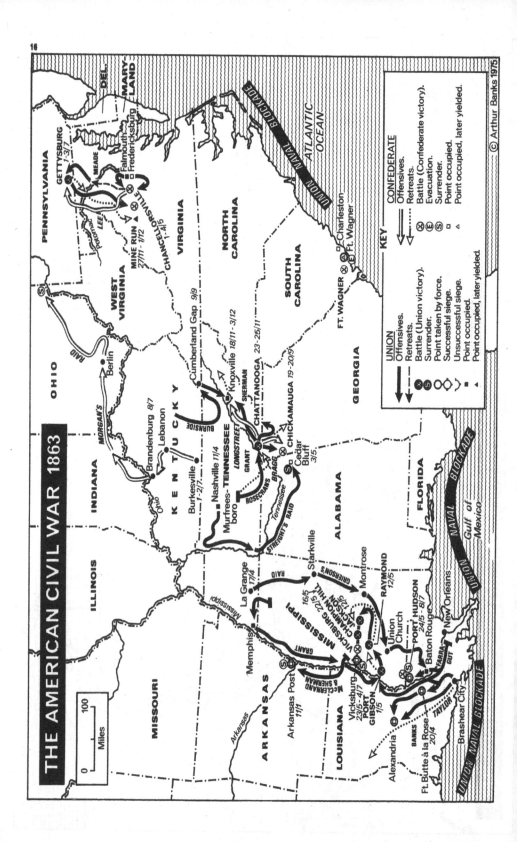

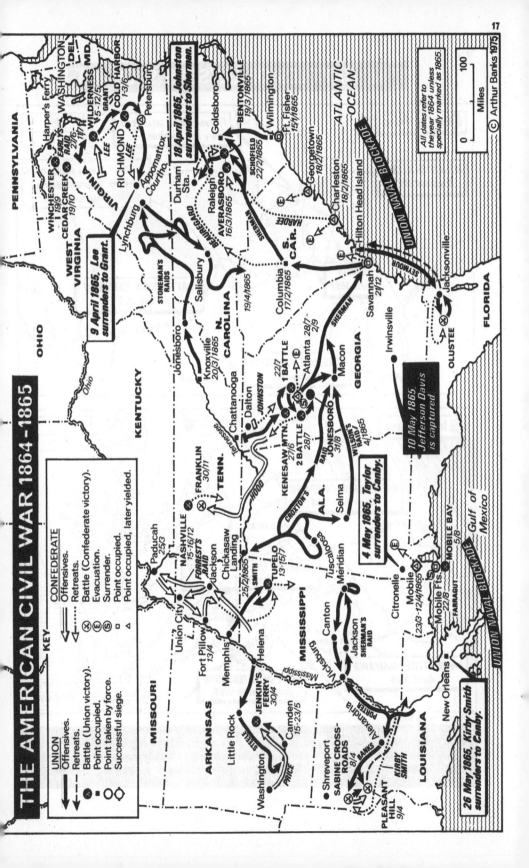

THE AMERICAN CIVIL WAR 1864–1865

17

KEY

UNION
Offensives.
Retreats.

CONFEDERATE
Offensives.
Retreats.

⊗ Battle (Union victory).
⊗ Battle (Confederate victory).
Ⓔ Evacuation.
Ⓢ Surrender.
□ Point occupied.
△ Point occupied, later yielded.

●▪○◇ Point taken by force.
Successful siege.

All dates refer to the year 1864 unless specially marked as 1865.

0   100
Miles

© Arthur Banks 1975

9 April 1865, Lee surrenders to Grant.

18 April 1865, Johnston surrenders to Sherman.

10 May 1865, Jefferson Davis is captured.

4 May 1865, Taylor surrenders to Canby.

26 May 1865, Kirby Smith surrenders to Canby.

PENNSYLVANIA

OHIO

WEST VIRGINIA

VIRGINIA

MARYLAND

DEL.

Harper's Ferry

WASHINGTON

WINCHESTER 19/9

WEST CEDAR CREEK 19/10

EARLY'S RAID 27/6–11/7

WILDERNESS 5/5–12/6

GRANT

Petersburg

COLD HARBOR 1-3/6

RICHMOND

LEE

Appomattox Courtho.

Lynchburg

STONEMAN'S RAIDS

Salisbury

Durham Sta.

Raleigh

AVERASBORO 16/3/1865

BEAUREGARD

Goldsboro

BENTONVILLE 19/3/1865

SCHOFIELD 22/2/1865

Wilmington

Ft. Fisher 15/1/1865

ATLANTIC OCEAN

Georgetown 18/2/1865

Charleston 18/2/1865

HARDEE

Hilton Head Island

UNION NAVAL BLOCKADE

KENTUCKY

N. CAROLINA

S. CAR.

Columbia 17/2/1865

19/4/1865

Jonesboro

Knoxville 20/3/1865

Chattanooga

Dalton

JOHNSTON

KENESAW MTN. 27/6

1 BATTLE 22/7

2 BATTLE 28/7

Atlanta 2/9

SHERMAN

Macon

GEORGIA

WILSON'S RAID 4/1865

JONESBORO 31/8

CROXTON'S RAID

ALA.

Selma

Savannah 21/12

SEYMOUR

Jacksonville

FLORIDA

Irwinsville

OLUSTEE

TENN.

FRANKLIN 30/11

HOOD

NASHVILLE 15/16/12

FORREST'S RAID

Jackson

Chickasaw Landing

TUPELO 13-15/7

SMITH 25/2/1865

Paducah 25/3

Union City

Fort Pillow 13/4

Helena

Memphis

MISSISSIPPI

Vicksburg

Canton

Jackson

SHERMAN'S RAID

Meridian

Tuscaloosa

ALA.

Citronelle

Mobile

Mobile Fts. 23/3–12/4/1865

MOBILE BAY 5/8

FARRAGUT

Gulf of Mexico

UNION NAVAL BLOCKADE

MISSOURI

ARKANSAS

Little Rock

JENKIN'S FERRY 30/4

STEELE

Washington

Camden 15–23/5

PRICE

SABINE CROSS-ROADS 8/4

Shreveport

Alexandria

PORTER

BANKS

KIRBY SMITH

LOUISIANA

New Orleans

PLEASANT HILL 9/4

Ohio

Tennessee

Mississippi

THE BATTLES OF ULYSSES S. GRANT

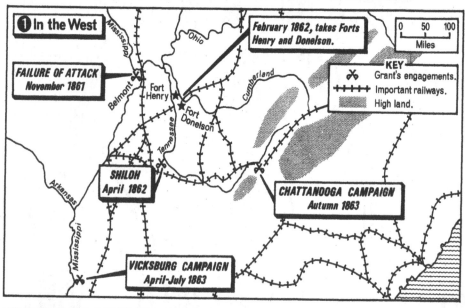

1 In the West

| 0 | 50 | 100 |

Miles

February 1862, takes Forts Henry and Donelson.

FAILURE OF ATTACK
November 1861

Fort Henry

Fort Donelson

KEY
✂ Grant's engagements.
╋╋╋ Important railways.
▓ High land.

SHILOH
April 1862

CHATTANOOGA CAMPAIGN
Autumn 1863

VICKSBURG CAMPAIGN
April–July 1863

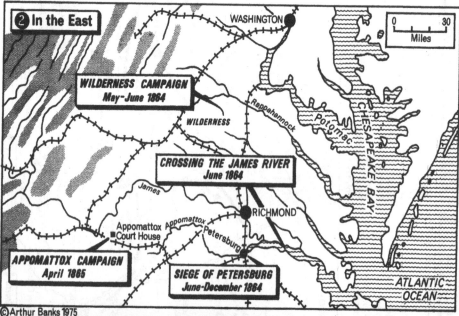

2 In the East

WASHINGTON

| 0 | 30 |

Miles

WILDERNESS CAMPAIGN
May–June 1864

WILDERNESS

CROSSING THE JAMES RIVER
June 1864

RICHMOND

Appomattox
Court House

APPOMATTOX CAMPAIGN
April 1865

SIEGE OF PETERSBURG
June–December 1864

ATLANTIC OCEAN

CHESAPEAKE BAY

© Arthur Banks 1975

Ulysses Simpson Grant (1822–1885) served as an infantry officer in the Mexican War but resigned from the army in 1854 following a period of heavy drinking. He volunteered for service in the Union army in 1861, and was speedily given command of an infantry regiment. Rapidly promoted brigadier-general, he became lieutenant-general in March 1864 and general-in-chief three days later. In 1868 he was elected president and served twice.

THE BATTLES OF WILLIAM T. SHERMAN

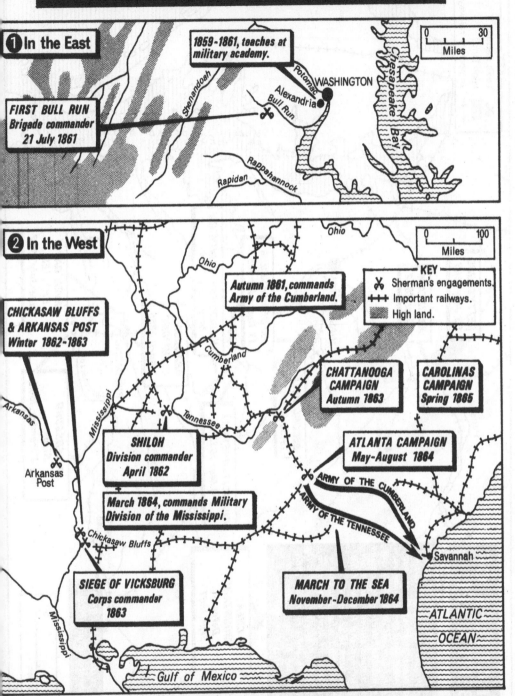

1 In the East

1859-1861, teaches at military academy.

Potomac

WASHINGTON

Alexandria

Bull Run

Shenandoah

Chesapeake Bay

FIRST BULL RUN
Brigade commander
21 July 1861

Rappahannock

Rapidan

30
Miles

2 In the West

Ohio

Ohio

100
Miles

Autumn 1861, commands Army of the Cumberland.

KEY
✂ Sherman's engagements.
+++ Important railways.
▓ High land.

CHICKASAW BLUFFS & ARKANSAS POST
Winter 1862-1863

Cumberland

CHATTANOOGA CAMPAIGN
Autumn 1863

CAROLINAS CAMPAIGN
Spring 1865

Arkansas

Mississippi

Tennessee

SHILOH
Division commander
April 1862

ATLANTA CAMPAIGN
May-August 1864

Arkansas Post

March 1864, commands Military Division of the Mississippi.

ARMY OF THE CUMBERLAND

ARMY OF THE TENNESSEE

Chickasaw Bluffs

Savannah

SIEGE OF VICKSBURG
Corps commander
1863

MARCH TO THE SEA
November-December 1864

ATLANTIC OCEAN

Mississippi

Gulf of Mexico

© Arthur Banks 1975

William Tecumseh Sherman (1820-1891) resigned from the army in 1853 and, after working as a banker and practising law, became superintendent of a military academy in 1859. In 1861 he volunteered for Federal service and was promoted to brigadier-general in August, major-general in May 1862, lieutenant-general in July 1866, and, as a full general, succeeded Grant as commander-in-chief in 1869. He held this post until 1883.

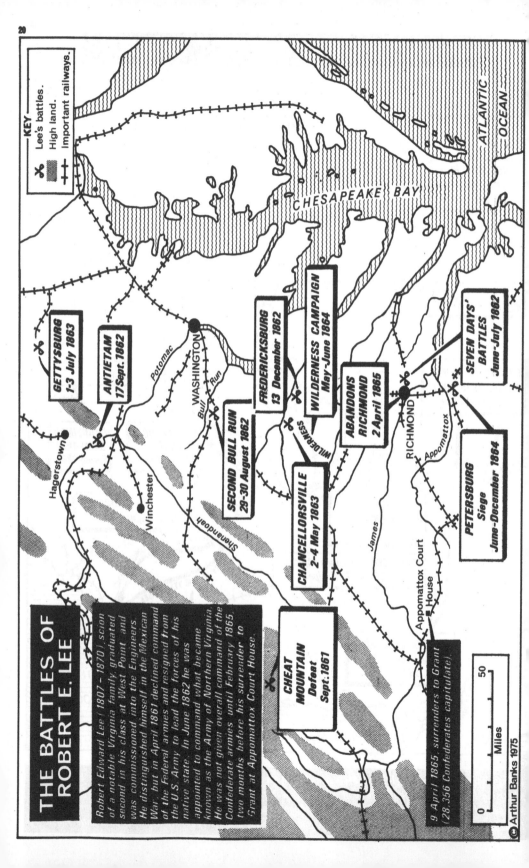

KEY
✕ Lee's battles.
▨ High land.
╅╅╅ Important railways.

THE BATTLES OF ROBERT E. LEE

Robert Edward Lee (1807–1870), scion of a notable Virginia family, graduated second in his class at West Point and was commissioned into the US Engineers. He distinguished himself in the Mexican War, but in April 1861 declined command of the Federal armies and resigned from the U.S. Army to lead the forces of his native state. In June 1862 he was appointed to command what became known as the Army of Northern Virginia. He was not given overall command of the Confederate armies until February 1855, two months before his surrender to Grant at Appomattox Court House.

CHESAPEAKE BAY

ATLANTIC OCEAN

GETTYSBURG
1-3 July 1863

ANTIETAM
17 Sept. 1862

FREDERICKSBURG
13 December 1862

WILDERNESS CAMPAIGN
May-June 1864

SEVEN DAYS'
BATTLES
June-July 1862

SECOND BULL RUN
29-30 August 1862

ABANDONS
RICHMOND
2 April 1865

CHANCELLORSVILLE
2-4 May 1863

PETERSBURG
Siege
June-December 1864

WASHINGTON

Potomac

Bull Run

WILDERNESS

RICHMOND

Appomattox

Hagerstown

Winchester

Shenandoah

James

Appomattox Court
House

CHEAT
MOUNTAIN
Defeat
Sept. 1861

9 April 1865, surrenders to Grant
(28,356 Confederates capitulate).

0   Miles   50

© Arthur Banks 1975

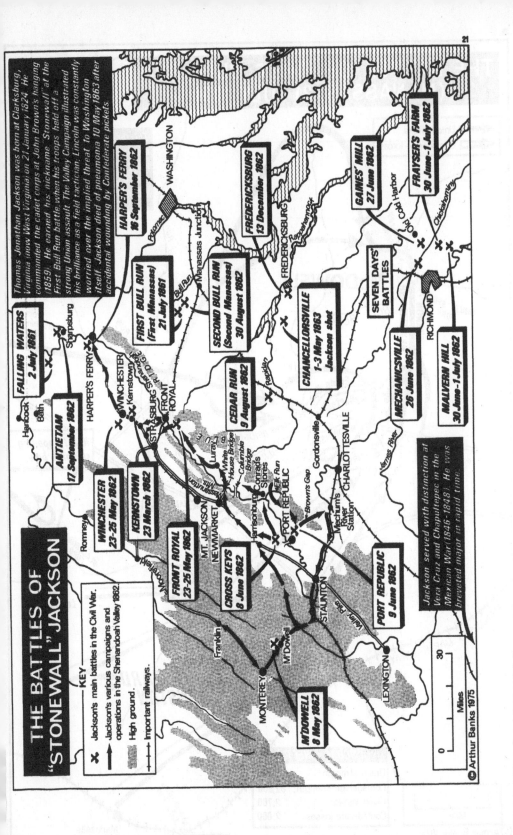

THE BATTLES OF "STONEWALL" JACKSON

KEY
✕ Jackson's main battles in the Civil War.

→ Jackson's various campaigns and operations in the Shenandoah Valley 1862.

▨ High ground.

+++ Important railways.

Thomas Jonathan Jackson was born at Clarksburg, Virginia (now West Virginia) on 21 January 1824. He commanded the cadet corps at John Brown's hanging 1859. He earned his nickname "Stonewall" at the First Bull Run battle, when his troops held off a strong Union assault. The Valley Campaign illustrated his brilliance as a field tactician. Lincoln was constantly worried over the implied threat to Washington itself. Jackson died of pneumonia 10 May 1863 after accidental wounding by Confederate pickets.

Jackson served with distinction at Vera Cruz and Chapultepec in the Mexican War (1846-1848). He was breveted major in rapid time.

FALLING WATERS 2 July 1861

ANTIETAM 17 September 1862

HARPER'S FERRY 16 September 1862

FIRST BULL RUN (First Manassas) 21 July 1861

SECOND BULL RUN (Second Manassas) 30 August 1862

FREDERICKSBURG 13 December 1862

GAINES' MILL 27 June 1862

FRAYSER'S FARM 30 June-1 July 1862

WINCHESTER 23-25 May 1862

KERNSTOWN 23 March 1862

CEDAR RUN 9 August 1862

CHANCELLORSVILLE 1-3 May 1863 Jackson shot

SEVEN DAYS' BATTLES

MECHANICSVILLE 26 June 1862

MALVERN HILL 30 June-1 July 1862

FRONT ROYAL 23-25 May 1862

CROSS KEYS 8 June 1862

PORT REPUBLIC 9 June 1862

McDOWELL 8 May 1862

© Arthur Banks 1975

Miles
0   30

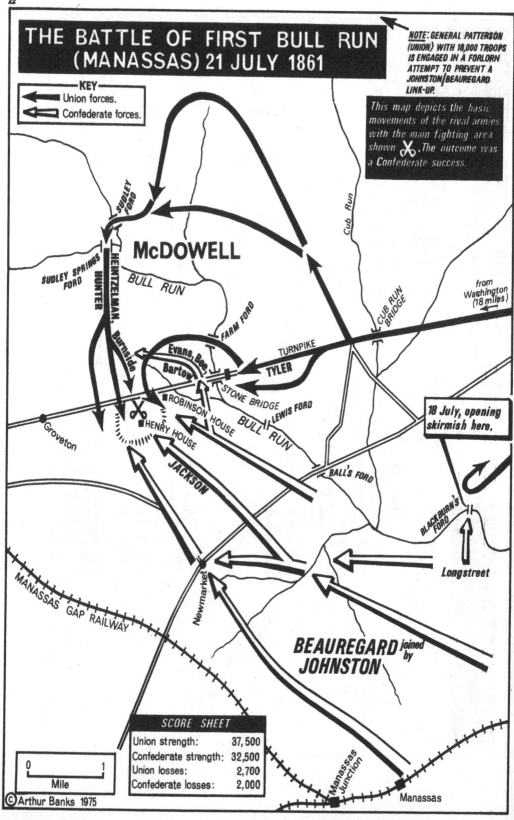

THE BATTLE OF SECOND BULL RUN (MANASSAS) 30 AUGUST 1862

Lee was determined to prevent a junction between the armies of Pope and McClellan. Sending Jackson north to distract Pope's attention from his main force, Lee (including Longstreet) followed several days later via the Thoroughfare Gap approach route. As Pope was engaging Jackson, Longstreet struck from the south-west. The result was a decisive Confederate victory.

SUDLEY FORD

SUDLEY SPRINGS FORD

BULL RUN

STONE BRIDGE

JACKSON

Groveton Ridge

POPE

BRANCH

YOUNG'S

HENRY HOUSE

GROVETON

unfinished railway line

TURNPIKE

Thoroughfare Gap

LONGSTREET

THE DECISIVE CONFEDERATE ASSAULT.

LEE

LEE'S APPROACH

DAWKINS BRANCH

to Richmond

KEY
Union forces.
Confederate forces.

0   1
Mile

© Arthur Banks 1975

SCORE SHEET	
Union strength:	70,000
Confederate strength:	50,000
Union casualties:	14,500
Confederate casualties:	9,500

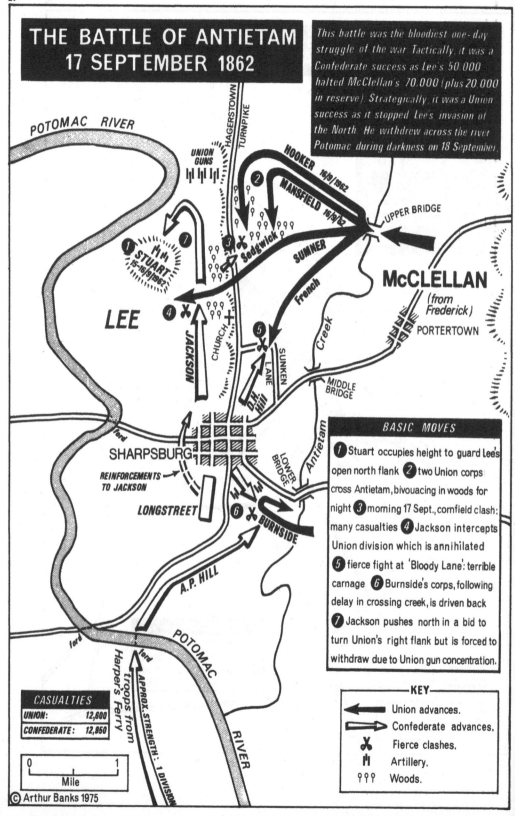

THE BATTLE OF ANTIETAM
17 SEPTEMBER 1862

This battle was the bloodiest one-day struggle of the war. Tactically, it was a Confederate success as Lee's 50,000 halted McClellan's 70,000 (plus 20,000 in reserve). Strategically, it was a Union success as it stopped Lee's invasion of the North. He withdrew across the river Potomac during darkness on 18 September.

POTOMAC RIVER

HAGERSTOWN TURNPIKE

UNION GUNS

HOOKER 16/9/1862

MANSFIELD 16/9/62

UPPER BRIDGE

STUART 15-16/9/1962

Sedgwick

SUMNER

French

Antietam Creek

McCLELLAN
(from Frederick)

PORTERTOWN

LEE

JACKSON

CHURCH

Sunken LANE

D.H. Hill

MIDDLE BRIDGE

SHARPSBURG

REINFORCEMENTS TO JACKSON

LONGSTREET

LOWER BRIDGE

BURNSIDE

Antietam

A.P. HILL

POTOMAC RIVER

ford

troops from Harper's Ferry

APPROX. STRENGTH: 1 DIVISION

BASIC MOVES

1 Stuart occupies height to guard Lee's open north flank **2** two Union corps cross Antietam, bivouacing in woods for night **3** morning 17 Sept., cornfield clash: many casualties **4** Jackson intercepts Union division which is annihilated **5** fierce fight at 'Bloody Lane': terrible carnage **6** Burnside's corps, following delay in crossing creek, is driven back **7** Jackson pushes north in a bid to turn Union's right flank but is forced to withdraw due to Union gun concentration.

CASUALTIES

UNION:	12,600
CONFEDERATE:	12,950

0 — 1
Mile

© Arthur Banks 1975

KEY

← Union advances.
⇨ Confederate advances.
✂ Fierce clashes.
⛿ Artillery.
♀♀♀ Woods.

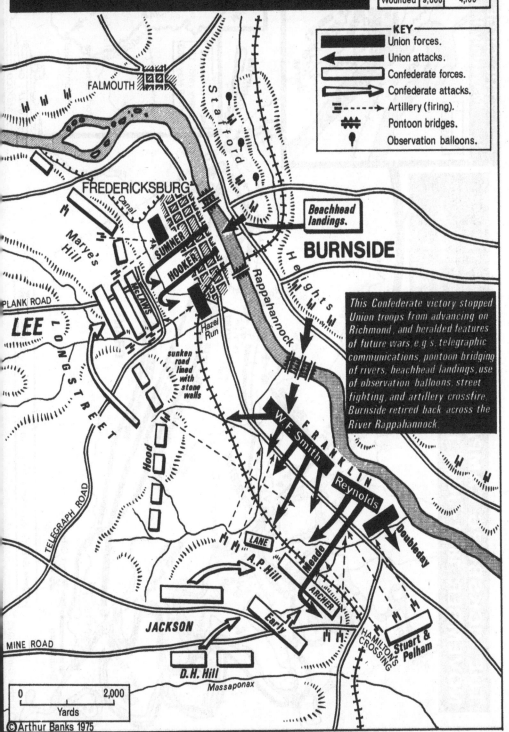

THE BATTLE OF FREDERICKSBURG
13 DECEMBER 1862

SCORE SHEET

LOSSES	Union	Confederate
Killed	1,300	600
Wounded	9,600	4,100

KEY

- Union forces.
- Union attacks.
- Confederate forces.
- Confederate attacks.
- Artillery (firing).
- Pontoon bridges.
- Observation balloons.

FALMOUTH

Stafford

FREDERICKSBURG

Canal

Marye's Hill

SUMNER

HOOKER

Beachhead landings.

BURNSIDE

Heights

Rappahannock

PLANK ROAD

LEE

McLAWS

LONGSTREET

Hazel Run

sunken road lined with stone walls

This Confederate victory stopped Union troops from advancing on Richmond, and heralded features of future wars, e.g's. telegraphic communications, pontoon bridging of rivers, beachhead landings, use of observation balloons, street fighting, and artillery crossfire. Burnside retired back across the River Rappahannock.

W.F. Smith

F R A N K L I N

Hood

Reynolds

TELEGRAPH ROAD

LANE

A.P. Hill

Meade

ARCHER

Doubleday

JACKSON

Early

HAMILTON'S CROSSING

Stuart & Pelham

MINE ROAD

D.H. Hill

Massaponax

0   2,000

Yards

© Arthur Banks 1975

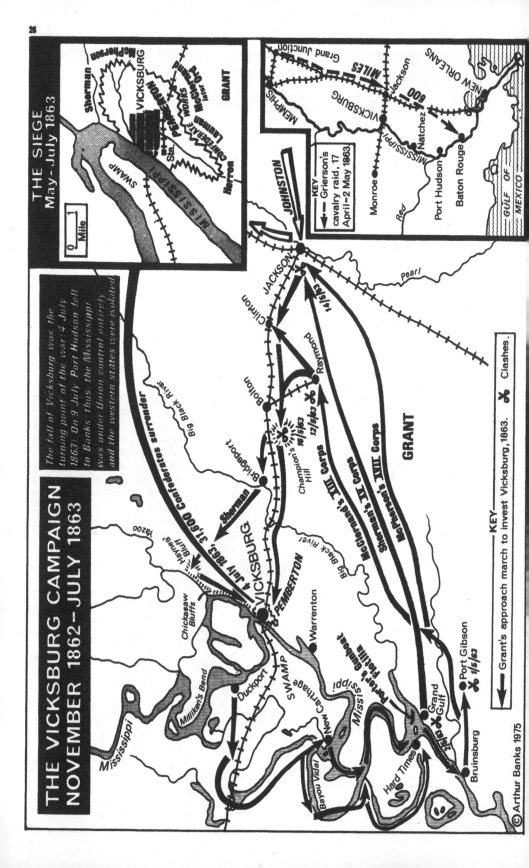

THE VICKSBURG CAMPAIGN NOVEMBER 1862–JULY 1863

THE SIEGE May–July 1863

The fall of Vicksburg was the turning point of the war 4 July 1863. On 9 July Port Hudson fell to Banks; thus the Mississippi was under Union control entirely and the western states were isolated.

KEY
— Grierson's cavalry raid, 17 April–2 May 1863.

KEY
—— Grant's approach march to invest Vicksburg, 1863. ✕ Clashes.

© Arthur Banks 1975

THE BATTLE OF CHANCELLORSVILLE 1-6 MAY 1863

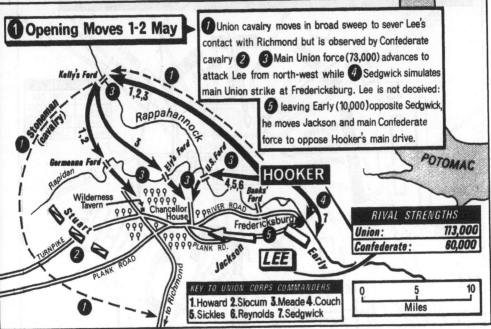

① Opening Moves 1-2 May

❶ Union cavalry moves in broad sweep to sever Lee's contact with Richmond but is observed by Confederate cavalry ❷ ❸ Main Union force (73,000) advances to attack Lee from north-west while ❹ Sedgwick simulates main Union strike at Fredericksburg. Lee is not deceived: ❺ leaving Early (10,000) opposite Sedgwick, he moves Jackson and main Confederate force to oppose Hooker's main drive.

RIVAL STRENGTHS

Union:	113,000
Confederate:	60,000

KEY TO UNION CORPS COMMANDERS
1. Howard 2. Slocum 3. Meade 4. Couch
5. Sickles 6. Reynolds 7. Sedgwick

0   5   10
Miles

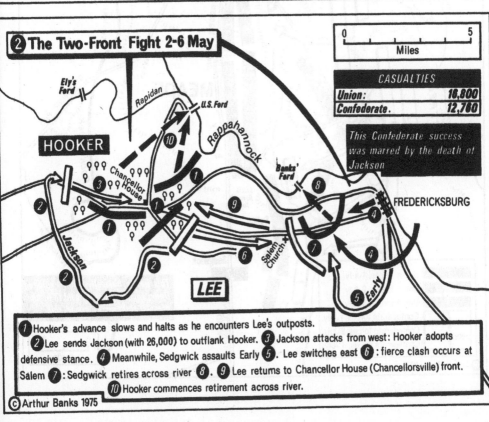

② The Two-Front Fight 2-6 May

0   5
Miles

CASUALTIES

Union:	16,800
Confederate:	12,760

This Confederate success was marred by the death of Jackson

❶ Hooker's advance slows and halts as he encounters Lee's outposts. ❷ Lee sends Jackson (with 26,000) to outflank Hooker. ❸ Jackson attacks from west: Hooker adopts defensive stance. ❹ Meanwhile, Sedgwick assaults Early ❺. Lee switches east ❻: fierce clash occurs at Salem ❼: Sedgwick retires across river ❽. ❾ Lee returns to Chancellor House (Chancellorsville) front. ❿ Hooker commences retirement across river.

© Arthur Banks 1975

THE BATTLE OF GETTYSBURG 1-3 JULY 1863

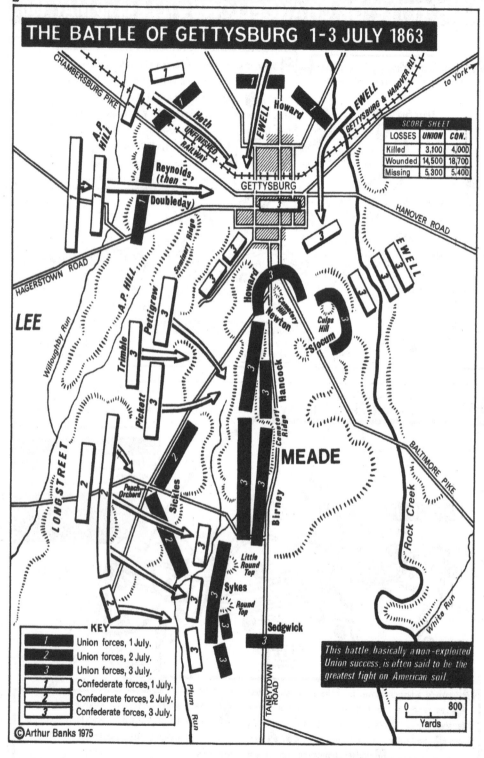

CHAMBERSBURG PIKE

to York

A.P. HILL

EWELL

Howard

EWELL

GETTYSBURG & HANOVER RLY

Heth

UNFINISHED RAILWAY

SCORE SHEET		
LOSSES	UNION	CON.
Killed	3,100	4,000
Wounded	14,500	18,700
Missing	5,300	5,400

Reynolds (then Doubleday)

GETTYSBURG

HANOVER ROAD

EWELL

HAGERSTOWN ROAD

Seminary Ridge

Howard

Cemetery Hill

Newton

Culps Hill

Slocum

A.P. HILL

LEE

Willoughby Run

Pettigrew

Trimble

Pickett

Cemetery Ridge

Hancock

MEADE

BALTIMORE PIKE

Peach Orchard

Sickles

Birney

Rock Creek

LONGSTREET

Little Round Top

Sykes

Round Top

Plum Run

Sedgwick

White Run

TANEYTOWN ROAD

KEY

1	Union forces, 1 July.
2	Union forces, 2 July.
3	Union forces, 3 July.
1	Confederate forces, 1 July.
2	Confederate forces, 2 July.
3	Confederate forces, 3 July.

This battle, basically a non-exploited Union success, is often said to be the greatest fight on American soil.

0   800
Yards

© Arthur Banks 1975

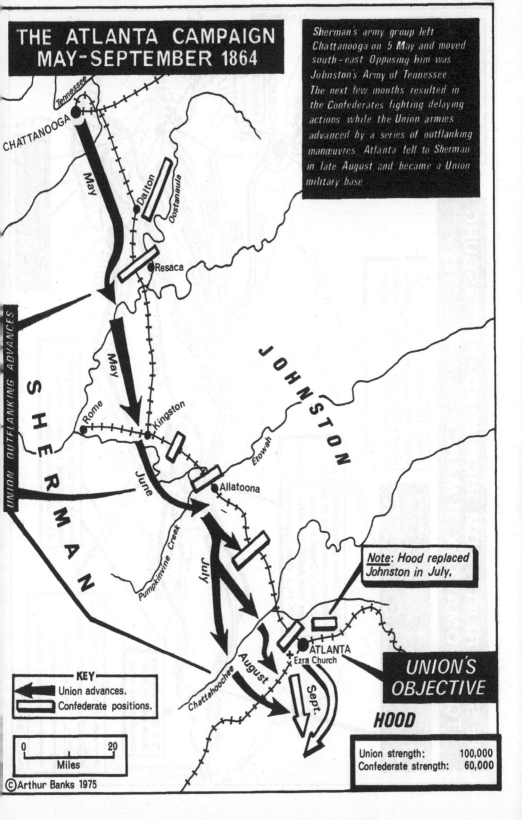

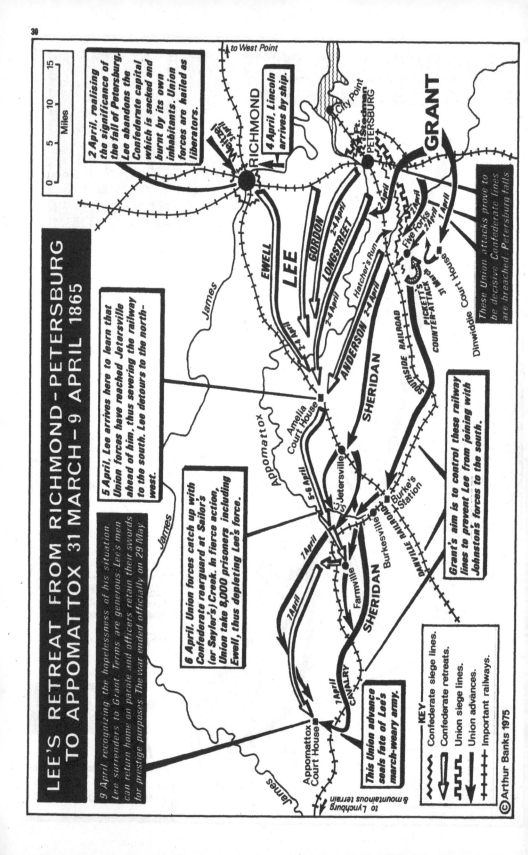

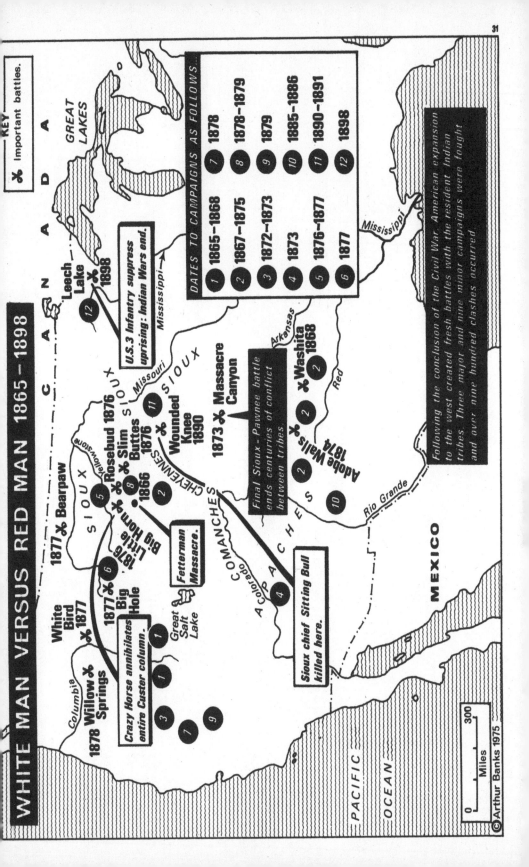

WHITE MAN VERSUS RED MAN 1865 – 1898

KEY
✠ Important battles.

DATES TO CAMPAIGNS AS FOLLOWS:

1 1865–1868	**7** 1878
2 1867–1875	**8** 1878–1879
3 1872–1873	**9** 1879
4 1873	**10** 1885–1886
5 1876–1877	**11** 1890–1891
6 1877	**12** 1898

Following the conclusion of the Civil War, American expansion to the west created fresh battles with the resident Indian tribes. Three major and nine minor campaigns were fought and over nine hundred clashes occurred.

GREAT LAKES

CANADA

Leech Lake ✠ 1898 **12**

U.S.3 Infantry suppress uprising: Indian Wars end.

Mississippi →

Missouri

SIOUX

SIOUX

1873 ✠ Massacre Canyon

Final Sioux – Pawnee battle ends centuries of conflict between tribes.

Rosebud 1876 ✠
11 Wounded Knee 1890 ✠
Slim Buttes 1876 ✠ **8**
1866 ●
2
CHEYENNES

Arkansas

✠ Washita 1868 **2**

Red

✠ Adobe Walls 1874 **2**

Bearpaw 1877 ✠

Yellowstone

5

Little Big Horn 1876 ✠ **6**

Fetterman Massacre.

COMANCHES

A P A C H E S

Colorado

4

Sioux chief Sitting Bull killed here.

Rio Grande

MEXICO

10

White Bird ✠ 1877

1878 ✠ Willow Springs
Columbia

Big Hole ✠ 1877 **9**

Crazy Horse annihilates entire Custer column.

Great Salt Lake

1
1
3
7
9

PACIFIC OCEAN

0   Miles   300

© Arthur Banks 1975

III
STRIFE & ALIGNMENTS

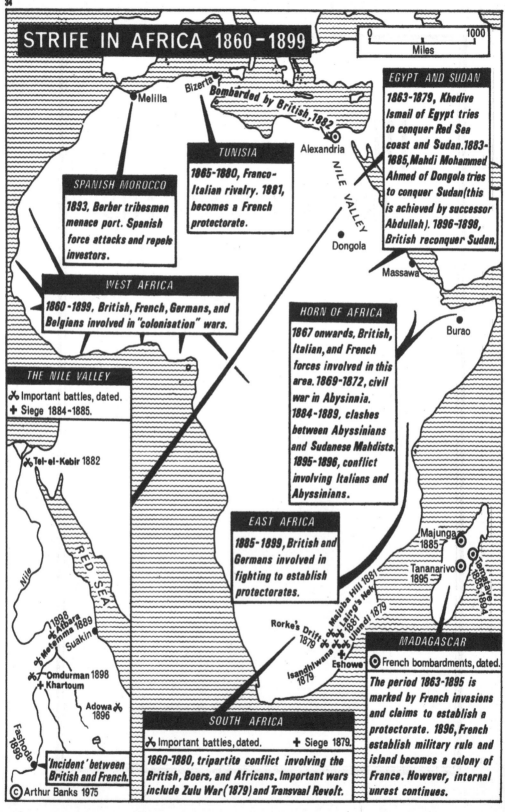

STRIFE IN AFRICA 1860-1899

0   1000
Miles

Melilla

Bizerta

Bombarded by British, 1882

Alexandria

EGYPT AND SUDAN

1863-1879, Khedive Ismail of Egypt tries to conquer Red Sea coast and Sudan. 1883-1885, Mahdi Mohammed Ahmed of Dongola tries to conquer Sudan (this is achieved by successor Abdullah). 1896-1898, British reconquer Sudan.

NILE VALLEY

TUNISIA

1865-1880, Franco-Italian rivalry. 1881, becomes a French protectorate.

SPANISH MOROCCO

1893, Berber tribesmen menace port. Spanish force attacks and repels investors.

Dongola

Massawa

WEST AFRICA

1860-1899, British, French, Germans, and Belgians involved in "colonisation" wars.

HORN OF AFRICA

1867 onwards, British, Italian, and French forces involved in this area. 1869-1872, civil war in Abysinnia. 1884-1889, clashes between Abyssinians and Sudanese Mahdists. 1895-1896, conflict involving Italians and Abyssinians.

Burao

THE NILE VALLEY

⚔ Important battles, dated.
✚ Siege 1884-1885.

⚔ Tel-el-Kebir 1882

RED SEA

Nile

1898
⚔ Atbara
⚔ Metemma 1889
Suakin

⚔ Omdurman 1898
✚ Khartoum

Adowa ⚔
1896

Fashoda
1898

'Incident' between British and French.

EAST AFRICA

1885-1899, British and Germans involved in fighting to establish protectorates.

Majunga
1885

Tananarivo
1895

Tamatave
1885, 1894

Majuba Hill 1881
Laing's Nek 1881
Rorke's Drift ⚔ ⚔ Ulundi 1879
1879
✚
Isandhlwana   Eshowe
1879

MADAGASCAR

⊙ French bombardments, dated.

The period 1863-1895 is marked by French invasions and claims to establish a protectorate. 1896, French establish military rule and island becomes a colony of France. However, internal unrest continues.

SOUTH AFRICA

⚔ Important battles, dated.   ✚ Siege 1879.

1860-1880, tripartite conflict involving the British, Boers, and Africans. Important wars include Zulu War (1879) and Transvaal Revolt.

© Arthur Banks 1975

STRIFE IN AFRICA 1899-1914

0   1000
Miles

This map shows areas of local conflict numbered in chronological sequence.

5

Tripoli

Agadir

NORTHERN SAHARA
1900, French establish their authority in desert areas (e.g. oases).

WADAI
1909-11, conquered by French.

MAURETANIA
1908-9, conquered by French.

NORTHERN NIGERIA
1900-3, British conquer area.

16

N.W. NIGERIA
1906, insurrection in Sokoto.

BAGIRMI
1900, French defeat R. Zobeir.

14   **6**

17

4

SOMALILAND
1899-1900, Mohammed ben Abdullah clashes with British, Italians, Ethiopians.

1

3

9

12

10

GOLD COAST
1900, uprising: British suppress Ushantis.

FRENCH CONGO
1905, uprising.

SOUTHERN NIGERIA
1904, insurrection.

CAMEROON
1904-5, Germans suppress insurrection.

13

ANGOLA
1907, uprising (inspired by Herero uprising in German S.W. Africa).

15

7

ANGOLA
1902, uprising suppressed by Portuguese.

8

GERMAN S.W. AFRICA
1903, Hottentot uprising.

11

2

GERMAN EAST AFRICA
1905, insurrection.

18

GERMAN S.W. AFRICA
1904-8, uprising (Herero tribe plus Hottentots).

SOUTH AFRICA
1914, Boer uprising.

SOUTH AFRICA
1899-1902, Boer War (see page   ).

© Arthur Banks 1975

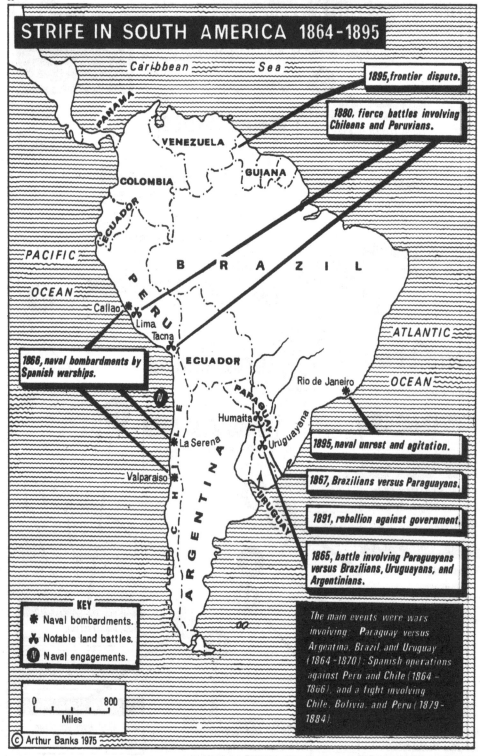

36

STRIFE IN SOUTH AMERICA 1864-1895

Caribbean Sea

PANAMA

VENEZUELA

COLOMBIA

GUIANA

ECUADOR

PACIFIC

OCEAN

B R A Z I L

PERU

Callao

Lima

Tacna

ECUADOR

ATLANTIC

Rio de Janeiro

OCEAN

1895, frontier dispute.

1880, fierce battles involving Chileans and Peruvians.

1866, naval bombardments by Spanish warships.

PARAGUAY

Humaita

Uruguayana

1895, naval unrest and agitation.

1867, Brazilians versus Paraguayans.

1891, rebellion against government.

1865, battle involving Paraguayans versus Brazilians, Uruguayans, and Argentinians.

La Serena

Valparaiso

C H I L E

A R G E N T I N A

URUGUAY

KEY
- Naval bombardments.
- Notable land battles.
- N Naval engagements.

0   800
Miles

© Arthur Banks 1975

The main events were wars involving: Paraguay versus Argentina, Brazil, and Uruguay (1864-1870); Spanish operations against Peru and Chile (1864-1866); and a fight involving Chile, Bolivia, and Peru (1879-1884).

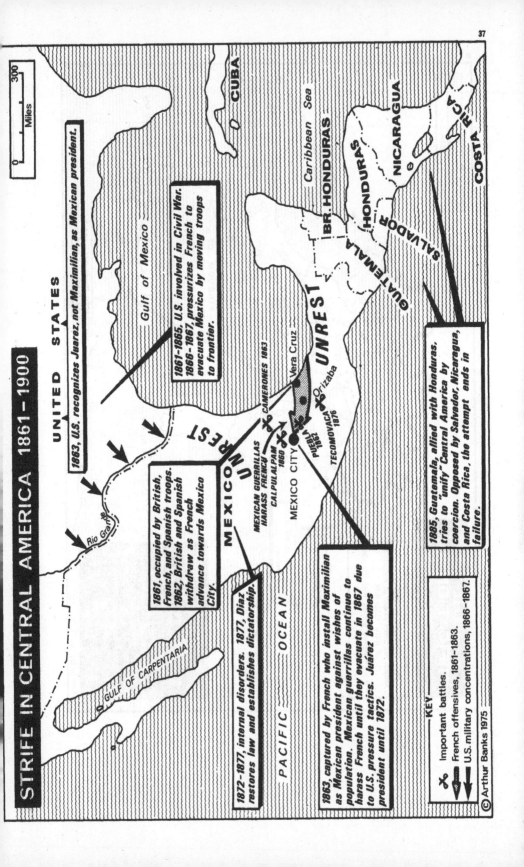

STRIFE IN CENTRAL AMERICA 1861–1900

1863, U.S. recognizes Juarez, not Maximilian, as Mexican president.

1861–1865, U.S. involved in Civil War. 1866–1867, pressurizes French to evacuate Mexico by moving troops to frontier.

1861, occupied by British, French, and Spanish troops. 1862, British and Spanish withdraw as French advance towards Mexico City.

1872–1877, internal disorders. 1877, Diaz restores law and establishes dictatorship.

1863, captured by French who install Maximilian as Mexican president against wishes of population. Mexican guerrillas continue to harass French until they evacuate in 1867 due to U.S. pressure tactics. Juárez becomes president until 1872.

1885, Guatemala, allied with Honduras, tries to "unify" Central America by coercion. Opposed by Salvador, Nicaragua, and Costa Rica, the attempt ends in failure.

UNITED STATES

Gulf of Mexico

Rio Grande

GULF OF CARPENTARIA

PACIFIC OCEAN

MEXICO CITY

MEXICAN GUERRILLAS HARASS FRENCH

CALPULALPAM 1860

PUEBLA 1862

TECOMOVACA 1876

Orizaba

CAMERONES 1863

Vera Cruz

U N R E S T

M E X I C O   U N R E S T

Caribbean Sea

CUBA

BR. HONDURAS

GUATEMALA

SALVADOR

HONDURAS

NICARAGUA

COSTA RICA

KEY

Important battles.
French offensives, 1861–1863.
U.S. military concentrations, 1866–1867.

© Arthur Banks 1975

300
Miles
0

37

THE UNIFICATION OF ITALY

KEY:
- ✗ Important battles.
- Northern extent of Kingdom of Italy, 1866–1914.
- •••• States joined with Kingdom of Italy.

Miles 0 300

ADRIATIC SEA

MEDITERRANEAN SEA

APULIA

CALABRIA

ASPROMONTE 1862

MILAZZO 1860

CAMPANIA

BENEVENTO

PONTECORVO

ABRUZZI

VOLTURNO 1860

ROME 1862

PAPAL STATES

KINGDOM OF THE TWO SICILIES

SICILY

Marsala

SARDINIA

CORSICA

KINGDOM OF SARDINIA

Genoa

GARIBALDI

LOMBARDY

VENETIA

PARMA

MODENA

LUCCA

TUSCANY

PIEDMONT

SAVOY

NICE

1860, Garibaldi and the 'Thousand' land here.

1859, allied with France.

In 1859 the Kingdom of Sardinia supported by France went to war to drive Austria out of Italy. Victories at Magenta and Solferino and Garibaldi's successes in the south encouraged revolutionary activities. These were followed by the collapse of most governments south of the River Po. In 1861 the Kingdom of Italy was proclaimed under Savoy excluding Venetia and Rome, these were annexed to Italy in 1866 and 1870 respectively.

© Arthur Banks 1975

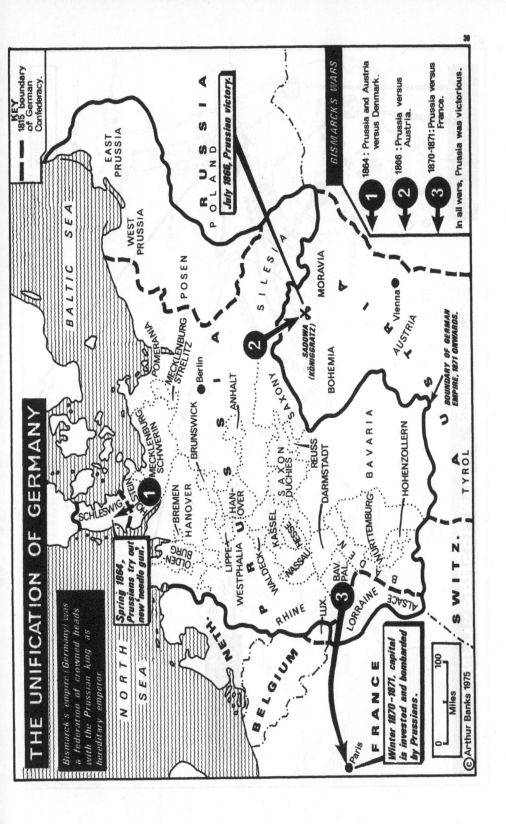

THE UNIFICATION OF GERMANY

Bismarck's empire (Germany) was a federation of crowned heads with the Prussian king as hereditary emperor.

KEY

— — 1815 boundary of German Confederacy.

BISMARCK'S WARS

1 1864 : Prussia and Austria versus Denmark.

2 1866 : Prussia versus Austria.

3 1870-1871: Prussia versus France.

In all wars, Prussia was victorious.

July 1866, Prussian victory.

Spring 1864, Prussians try out new needle gun.

Winter 1870-1871, capital is invested and bombarded by Prussians.

BOUNDARY OF GERMAN EMPIRE, 1871 ONWARDS.

0   100
Miles

© Arthur Banks 1975

39

40

THE FRANCO–PRUSSIAN WAR 1870–1871

PRUSSIAN CONCENTRATIONS
JULY 1870

Mannheim

Coblenz Rhine Bingen

G E R M A N Y
(Prussia in 1870)

② ③

THREE ARMIES

Saarbrücken

①

Trier

LUX.

NETH.

B E L G I U M

Lille

St. Quentin
BAPAUME

ST. QUENTIN

Abbeville
Somme

Beauvais

Dieppe

Le Havre

Rouen

Seine

ENGLISH CHANNEL

FRENCH
CONCENTRATION

ALSACE

WÖRTH

METZ (vicinity)

SPICHERN

GRAVELOTTE
ST. PRIVAT

Lorraine

Moselle

SEDAN

MAIN BREAKTHROUGH

Châlons

MAIN DRIVES

Oise Marne

Paris

Besieged for five months.
Despite three sorties,capital
surrenders in January 1871.

Toul

Épinal

Chaumont

Châtillon

Troyes

Seine Yonne

F R A N C E

PATAY

LE MANS

Tours Loire

Dijon NUITS ST.
GEORGES

EIGHT CORPS

Rhine Basle

S W I T Z.

Miles
0   50

KEY
German advances.
French provincial armies.
Important battles.

© Arthur Banks 1975

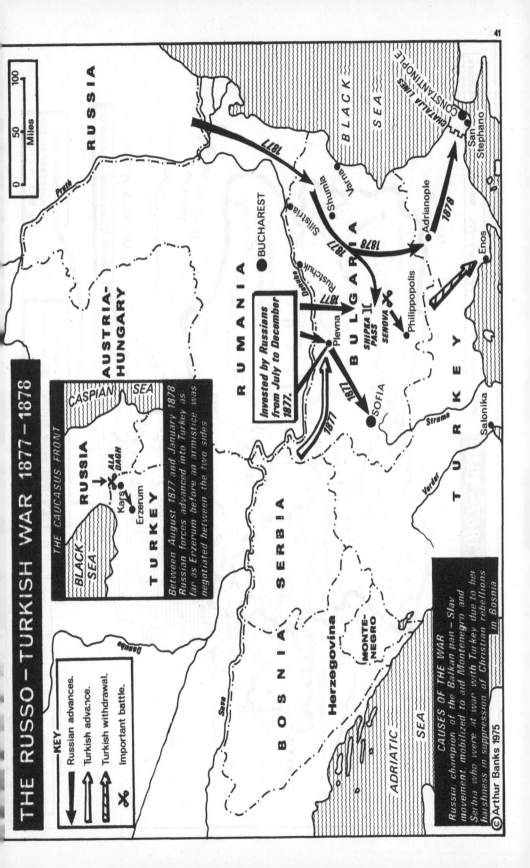

THE RUSSO–TURKISH WAR 1877–1878

KEY
Russian advances.
Turkish advance.
Turkish withdrawal.
Important battle.

THE CAUCASUS FRONT

CASPIAN SEA

RUSSIA

Kars • ✗ ALA DAGH
Erzerum •

TURKEY

BLACK SEA

Between August 1877 and January 1878 Russian forces advanced into Turkey as far as Erzerum before an armistice was negotiated between the two sides

RUSSIA

Pruth

AUSTRIA-HUNGARY

RUMANIA

• BUCHAREST

Danube
Silistria
Rustchuk • 1877

Shumla
Varna •

BLACK SEA

CHATALJA LINES

CONSTANTINOPLE

San Stephano

Adrianople •
1878

Enos •

Invested by Russians from July to December 1877.

Plevna •
1877
1877

BULGARIA

SHIPKA PASS
SENOVA ✗

• Phillippolis

1877
1877

SOFIA •

Struma

Salonika •

SERBIA

BOSNIA

Sava

Herzegovina

MONTE-NEGRO

TURKEY

Vardar

ADRIATIC SEA

CAUSES OF THE WAR
Russia champion of the Balkan pan–Slav movement mobilized to aid Montenegro and Serbia who were at war with Turkey due to her harshness in suppression of Christian rebellions in Bosnia

Danube

0   50   100
Miles

AUSTRIA - HUNGARY 1867 - 1918

KEY
▬▬ Frontier of Austria-Hungary 1918.
▬ ▬ ▬ Kingdom of Hungary.

RUSSIA

GERMANY

Eger
Prague
BOHEMIA
Pilsen
Elbe
SILESIA
Brünn
MORAVIA
Cracow
Teschen
Pozsony
Tarnopol
Czernowitz
Lemberg
Przemysl
GALICIA
Kassa
Miskolcz
Debreczen
Kolozsvar
TRANSYLVANIA
Brasso
Maros
Temesvar
Orsova
Danube
ROUMANIA (Rumania)

LOWER AUSTRIA
Vienna
Linz
UPPER AUSTRIA
Budapest
Szeged
H U N G A R Y
Pecs
Danube
Drava
Graz
STYRIA
CARINTHIA
CARNIOLA
Klagenfurt
Salzburg
Innsbruck
VORARLBERG
TYROL
Trient
SWITZ.
GORIZIA-GRADISCA
ISTRIA
Trieste
Fiume
Pola
Po
I T A L Y
ADRIATIC SEA
Spalato
Ragusa
DALMATIA
CROATIA
SLAVONIA
Sava
BOSNIA
Sarajevo
HERZEGOVINA
MONTE-NEGRO
SANJAK OF NOVIBAZAR
ALBANIA
SERBIA
BULGARIA

1878-1912, occupied by Austria.

Established with independent status in 1913.

Until 1878, part of Ottoman Empire; 1878-1908, under Austria: 1908, annexed to Austria.

Miles
0   300

© Arthur Banks 1975

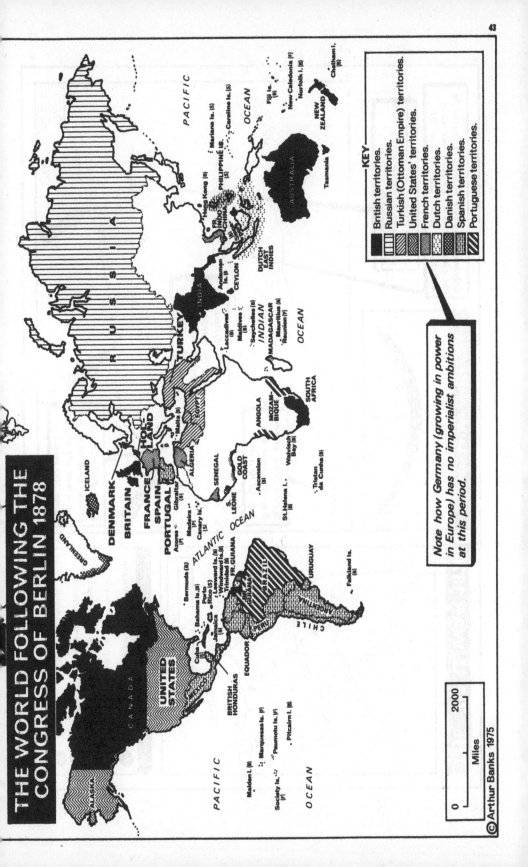

THE WORLD FOLLOWING THE CONGRESS OF BERLIN 1878

KEY

- British territories.
- Russian territories.
- Turkish (Ottoman Empire) territories.
- United States' territories.
- French territories.
- Dutch territories.
- Danish territories.
- Spanish territories.
- Portuguese territories.

Note how Germany (growing in power in Europe) has no imperialist ambitions at this period.

© Arthur Banks 1975

0   2000
Miles

THE ZULU WAR 1879

Cetewayo (the Zulu chief) is defeated in decisive battle which ends war. Zulu losses total 2,000: English lose 150.

British column is besieged by Zulus who withdraw when reinforcements arrive.

ZULU BATTLE FORMATION

HORN

CHEST

DIRECTION OF ATTACK

HORN

4,000 British and native troops are annihilated in a surprise Zulu raid.

18,000 Zulus attack British column but lose 1,200 men.

5,000 Zulus attack British base camp but are driven off after losing 300 men.

ESHOWE

ULUNDI

KAMBULA

ISANDHLWANA

RORKE'S DRIFT

BRITISH

BRITISH

BRITISH

Umfolozi

Black

White

Tugela Drift

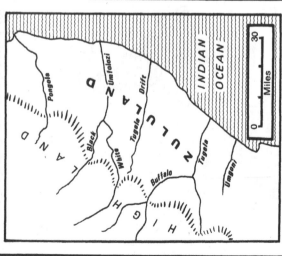

ZULU LAND

Pongola

Umfolozi

Black

White

Tugela Drift

Tugela

Buffalo

Umgeni

INDIAN OCEAN

0   30
Miles

MAIN EVENTS

1 22 JANUARY: Battle of Isandhlwana.
2 22/23 JANUARY: Battle of Rorke's Drift.
3 JANUARY-APRIL: Siege of Eshowe.
4 29 MARCH: Battle of Kambula.
5 4 JULY: Battle of Ulundi.

© Arthur Banks 1975

45

'SCRAMBLE FOR AFRICA' PRE-1914

This map illustrates that Britain and France led the race to colonize Africa.

THE FASHODA INCIDENT

In 1898, a French force (exploratory and military) reaches here on the Nile. Britain threatens France with war unless force withdraws: this occurs in November.

ATLANTIC OCEAN

SPANISH MOROCCO

ALGERIA

TRIPOLI (LIBYA)

EGYPT

ANGLO-EGYPTIAN SUDAN

FRENCH SOMALILAND

MOROCCO

RIO DE ORO

FRENCH WEST AFRICA

SENEGAL
GAMBIA
PORT. GUINEA
SIERRA LEONE
LIBERIA
GOLD COAST
TOGO
NIGERIA
SP. GUINEA
KAMERUN
Congo
FRENCH EQUATORIAL AFRICA

ABYSSINIA
ER ... BR. SOM.

Fashoda

BELGIAN CONGO

UGANDA
BR. EAST AFRICA

Free from European colonization.

ATLANTIC OCEAN

ANGOLA

GERMAN EAST AFRICA

Free from European colonization.

N. RHODESIA
S. RHOD.
NYASALAND

MADAGASCAR

GERMAN S.W. AFRICA

BECH.
TRANS VAAL
O.F.S.
SWAZILAND
NATAL
SOUTH AFRICA

MOZAMBIQUE

INDIAN OCEAN

KEY
British-controlled territories.
French-controlled territories.
German-controlled territories.
Italian-controlled territories.
Portuguese-controlled territories.
Belgian-controlled territory.
Spanish-controlled territories.
Uncontrolled by Europeans.

0   1000
Miles

© Arthur Banks 1975

THE BATTLE OF TEL-EL-KEBIR 12–13 SEPTEMBER 1882

Following this British victory, the Egyptians were pursued to Cairo where they surrendered on 14 September

BRITISH

Royal Marine Artillery

HQ

CAVALRY

1 BRIGADE

2 BRIGADE

ROYAL ARTILLERY BRIGADE

4 BRIGADE

3 BRIGADE

NAVAL BRIGADE

INDIAN CONTINGENT

forward position

TRENCH

infantry   guns   infantry   guns   infantry

EGYPTIANS
(plus Sudanese)

D E S E R T

TEL-EL-KEBIR VILLAGE

Railway

Sweetwater Canal

to Cairo

LOCATION MAP

0   3,000
Yards

Mediterranean Sea

Port Said
Ismailia
Suez Canal
Suez

TEL-EL-KEBIR

CAIRO

E G Y P T

Nile

Alexandria

0   100
Miles

SCORE SHEET

British engaged: 13,000
British casualties: 457
Egyptians engaged: 25,000
Egyptian casualties: 2,803

© Arthur Banks 1975

46

THE BATTLE OF OMDURMAN 2 SEPTEMBER 1898

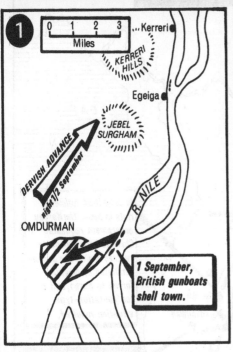

1

0 1 2 3
Miles

Kerreri

KERRERI HILLS

Egeiga

JEBEL SURGHAM

DERVISH ADVANCE night 1/2 September

OMDURMAN

R. NILE

1 September, British gunboats shell town.

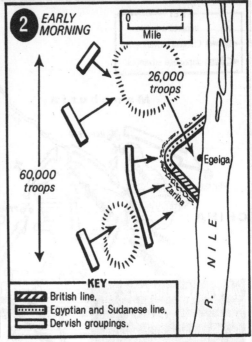

2 *EARLY MORNING*

0 1
Mile

26,000 troops

60,000 troops

Egeiga

Zariba

R. NILE

KEY
- British line.
- Egyptian and Sudanese line.
- Dervish groupings.

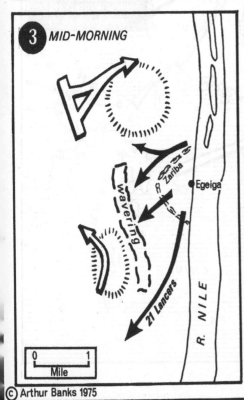

3 MID-MORNING

Zariba

wavering

Egeiga

21 Lancers

R. NILE

0 1
Mile

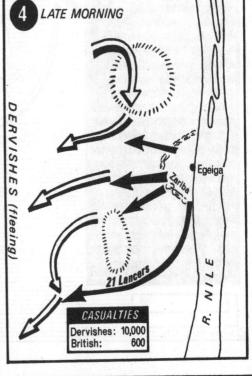

4 LATE MORNING

DERVISHES (fleeing)

Zariba

Egeiga

21 Lancers

R. NILE

CASUALTIES
Dervishes: 10,000
British: 600

© Arthur Banks 1975

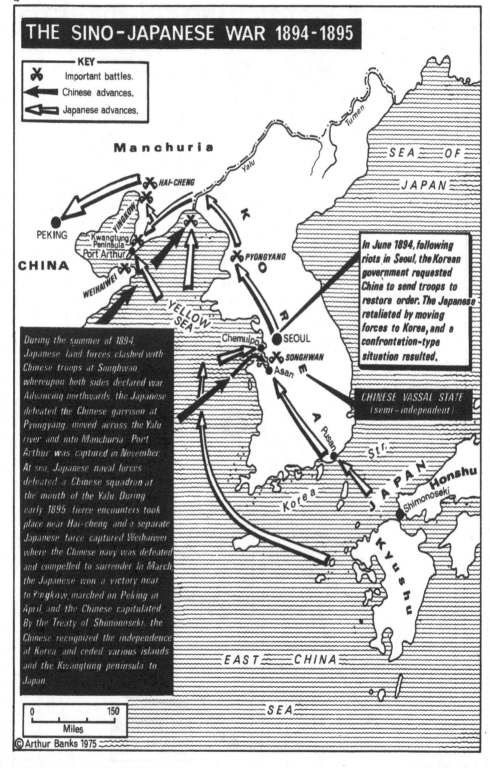

THE SINO-JAPANESE WAR 1894-1895

KEY
- ✗ Important battles.
- ⬅ Chinese advances.
- ⇦ Japanese advances.

Manchuria

SEA OF JAPAN

✗ HAI-CHENG

Yalu

Tumen

YINGKOW

PEKING

Kwangtung Peninsula
Port Arthur

CHINA

WEIHAIWEI

✗ PYONGYANG

K O R E A

YELLOW SEA

Chemulpo

SEOUL

✗ SONGHWAN

Asan

Pusan

Korea Str.

J A P A N

Shimonoseki

Honshu

Kyushu

EAST CHINA SEA

In June 1894, following riots in Seoul, the Korean government requested China to send troops to restore order. The Japanese retaliated by moving forces to Korea, and a confrontation-type situation resulted.

CHINESE VASSAL STATE (semi-independent)

During the summer of 1894, Japanese land forces clashed with Chinese troops at Songhwan, whereupon both sides declared war. Advancing northwards, the Japanese defeated the Chinese garrison at Pyongyang, moved across the Yalu river and into Manchuria. Port Arthur was captured in November. At sea, Japanese naval forces defeated a Chinese squadron at the mouth of the Yalu. During early 1895, fierce encounters took place near Hai-cheng and a separate Japanese force captured Weihaiwei where the Chinese navy was defeated and compelled to surrender. In March, the Japanese won a victory near to Yingkow, marched on Peking in April, and the Chinese capitulated. By the Treaty of Shimonoseki, the Chinese recognized the independence of Korea, and ceded various islands and the Kwangtung peninsula to Japan.

0   150
Miles

© Arthur Banks 1975

THE BOER (or SOUTH AFRICAN) WAR 1899-1902

The war was in two phases: the first (1899-1902) was an active open fight between Boers and British Empire troops which seemed to end with the victorious British advance of 1900. The second (1900-1902) was a guerrilla-style campaign by the Boers which caused the British to raid farms and homes and to force Boer women and children into concentration camps.

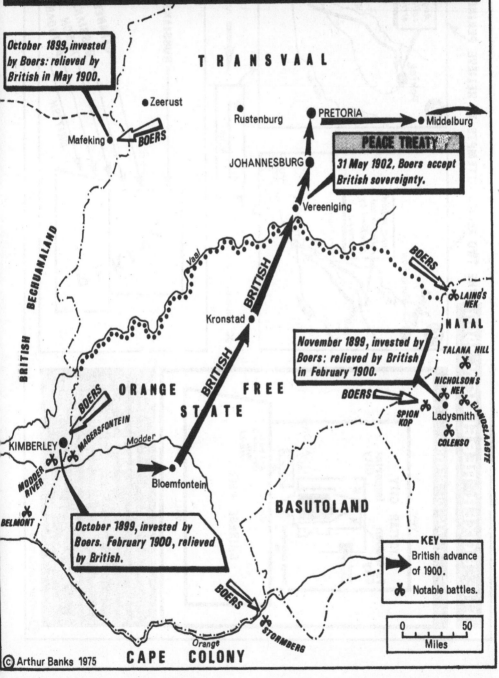

October 1899, invested by Boers: relieved by British in May 1900.

T R A N S V A A L

Zeerust
Rustenburg
PRETORIA
Middelburg
Mafeking
BOERS
JOHANNESBURG

PEACE TREATY
31 May 1902, Boers accept British sovereignty.

Vereeniging

BRITISH BECHUANALAND

Vaal

BRITISH

Kronstad

BOERS
LAING'S NEK

NATAL

November 1899, invested by Boers: relieved by British in February 1900.

TALANA HILL

NICHOLSON'S NEK

ORANGE FREE STATE

BOERS

BOERS
MAGERSFONTEIN
SPION KOP
Ladysmith
COLENSO
ELANDSLAAGTE

KIMBERLEY
Modder

MODDER RIVER
Bloemfontein

BELMONT

October 1899, invested by Boers. February 1900, relieved by British.

BASUTOLAND

KEY
British advance of 1900.
Notable battles.

BOERS
STORMBERG

0   50
Miles

© Arthur Banks 1975   CAPE COLONY
Orange

THE "BOXER" REBELLION 1900

THE TWO ALLIED ATTEMPTS TO RELIEVE PEKING

2

August, Allied relief force arrives here.

Peking

Pei Ho

Yang Tsun

Pietsang

TIENTSIN

Hun Ho

1

Peking

Tungchow

Pei Ho

Yang Tsun

TIENTSIN

Anping

Hun Ho

Taku

June, Allied relief force repulsed by Boxers.

→ Allied relief forces.

✂ Important battles.

0   30
Miles

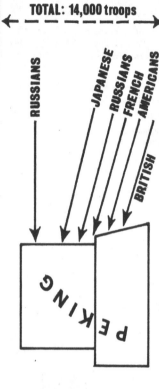

TOTAL: 14,000 troops

RUSSIANS

JAPANESE
RUSSIANS
FRENCH
AMERICANS

BRITISH

PEKING

PLAN OF PEKING

WALL

TARTAR CITY

Imperial City

Forbidden City

Palace

North Cathedral

LEGATION AREA

South Cathedral

BESIEGED DIPLOMATS AND FAMILIES

WALL

CHINESE CITY

WALL

For fifty-five days during the summer of 1900 some two thousand Europeans and Chinese Christians were besieged in Peking by a peasant army known as "Boxers" (Society of Righteous Harmonious Fists). Two attempts were made to relieve them by Allied (British, French American Russian and Japanese) forces, the first (in June) being unsuccessful, the second (in August) succeeding.

© Arthur Banks 1975

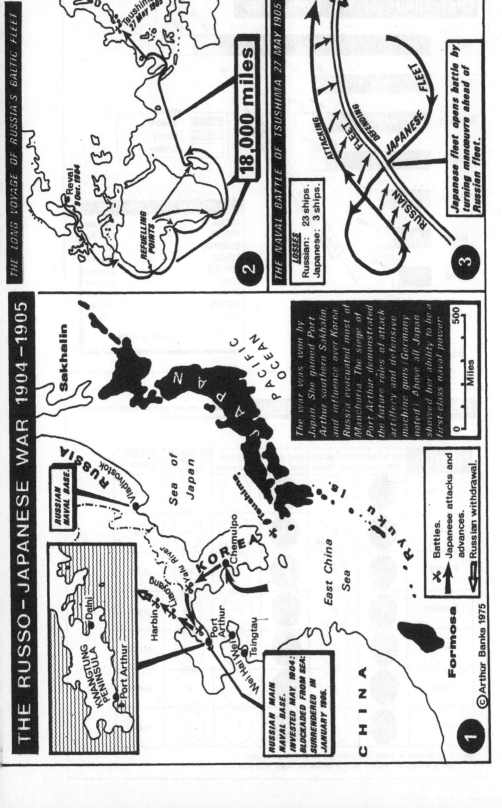

THE LONG VOYAGE OF RUSSIA'S BALTIC FLEET

Tsushima 27 May 1905

Reval 9 Oct. 1904

18,000 miles

REFUELLING POINTS

2

THE NAVAL BATTLE OF TSUSHIMA 27 MAY 1905

ATTACKING FLEET

DEFENDING FLEET

JAPANESE

RUSSIAN

LOSSES
Russian: 23 ships.
Japanese: 3 ships.

Japanese fleet opens battle by turning manoeuvre ahead of Russian fleet.

3

THE RUSSO–JAPANESE WAR 1904–1905

Sakhalin

J A P A N

PACIFIC OCEAN

Sea of Japan

RUSSIA

RUSSIAN NAVAL BASE.

Vladivostok

Tsushima

KOREA

Chemulpo

Yalu River

Liaoyang

Harbin

Port Arthur

Wei Hai Wei

Tsingtau

Dalni

KWANTUNG PENINSULA

Port Arthur

East China Sea

RYUKYU Is.

CHINA

Formosa

RUSSIAN MAIN NAVAL BASE. INVESTED MAY 1904: BLOCKADED FROM SEA: SURRENDERED IN JANUARY 1905.

The war was won by Japan. She gained Port Arthur, southern Sakhalin, and influence over Korea. Russia evacuated most of Manchuria. The siege of Port Arthur demonstrated the future roles of attack artillery and defensive machine guns (Germany noted). Above all Japan showed her ability to be a first-class naval power.

0   500
Miles

Battles.
Japanese attacks and advances.
Russian withdrawal.

© Arthur Banks 1975

1

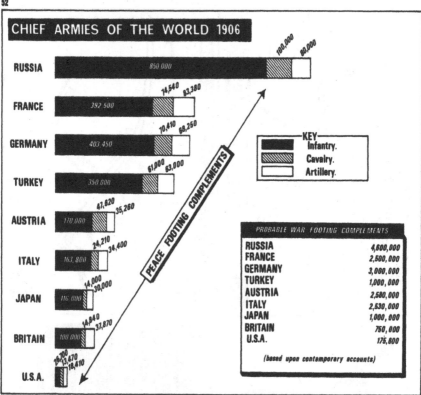

CHIEF NAVIES OF THE WORLD 1906

This was the year when the British 'Dreadnought' battleship was launched.

COUNTRY	BATTLESHIPS (first class)	BATTLESHIPS (other classes)	CRUISERS (first class)	CRUISERS (other classes)	DESTROYERS, SUBMARINES, M.T.B.'s	OFFICERS & MEN
BRITAIN	45	16	38	87	232	129,000
U.S.A.	19	11	7	14	47	37,000
FRANCE	11	19	10	37	271	28,500
GERMANY	18	13	6	24	103	33,500
RUSSIA	4	7	2	10	145	60,000
ITALY	4	9	3	17	61	26,800
JAPAN	10	4	9	17	72	36,000

Note: it was the axiom of British naval policy that her navy should roughly equal in strength the combined fleets of the next two largest naval powers.

THE ITALO–TURKISH WAR 1911–1912

SPAIN

ITALY

TURKEY

MEDITERRANEAN SEA

TUNISIA

ALGERIA

MOROCCO

FRENCH EMPIRE

TRIPOLI

MAIN CAUSE OF THE WAR. Italy wished to counterbalance the French empire in North Africa by conquering the Turkish colony of Tripoli/Libya

MEDITERRANEAN SEA

1911–1912, bombarded and occupied by Italians.

Tobruk

Derna

Benghazi

Homs

Tripoli

TUNISIA

ALGERIA

TRIPOLI

EGYPT

Due to the outbreak of the Balkan War Turkey sued for peace in October 1912

0 200
Miles

© Arthur Banks 1975

BLACK SEA

TURKEY

Dardanelles

April 1912, Italian naval units attack straits which are closed by Turks.

TURKEY

Dodecanese

Rhodes

May 1912, occupied by Italian naval forces.

CRISES IN NORTH AFRICA AND THE BALKANS 1905-1912

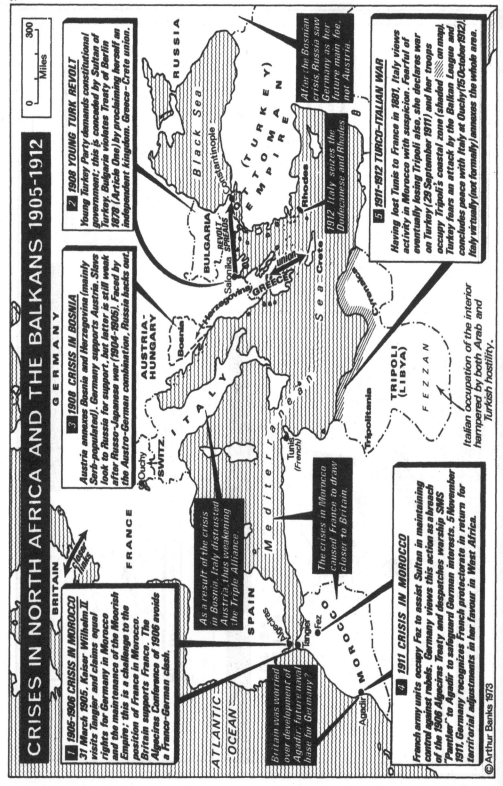

1 1905-1906 CRISIS IN MOROCCO

31 March 1905. Kaiser Wilhelm II visits Tangier and claims equal rights for Germany in Morocco and the maintenance of the Moorish Empire; this is a challenge to the position of France in Morocco. Britain supports France. The Algeciras Conference of 1906 avoids a Franco-German clash.

2 1908 YOUNG TURK REVOLT

Young Turkey Party demands constitutional government; this is conceded by Sultan of Turkey. Bulgaria violates Treaty of Berlin 1878 (Article One) by proclaiming herself an independent kingdom. Greece-Crete union.

3 1908 CRISIS IN BOSNIA

Austria annexes Bosnia and Herzegovina (mainly Serb-populated). Germany supports Austria. Slavs look to Russia for support, but latter is still weak after Russo-Japanese war (1904-1905). Faced by the Austro-German combination, Russia backs out.

After the Bosnian crisis, Russia saw Germany as her future main foe, not Austria.

5 1911-1912 TURCO-ITALIAN WAR

Having lost Tunis to France in 1881, Italy views activity in Morocco with suspicion. Fearful of eventually losing Tripoli also, she declares war on Turkey (29 September 1911) and her troops occupy Tripoli's coastal zone (shaded ▨▨ on map). Turkey fears an attack by the Balkan League and concludes peace with Italy at Ouchy (15 October 1912). Italy virtually (not formally) annexes the whole area.

1912. Italy seizes the Dodecanese and Rhodes.

As a result of the crisis in Bosnia, Italy distrusted Austria, thus weakening the Triple Alliance.

The crises in Morocco caused France to draw closer to Britain.

Italian occupation of the interior hampered by both Arab and Turkish hostility.

4 1911 CRISIS IN MOROCCO

French army units occupy Fez to assist Sultan in maintaining control against rebels. Germany views this action as a breach of the 1906 Algeciras Treaty and despatches warship SMS "Panther" to Agadir to safeguard German interests. 5 November 1911. Germany recognizes French protectorate in return for territorial adjustments in her favour in West Africa.

Britain was worried over development of Agadir: future naval base for Germany?

© Arthur Banks 1973

0   300
    Miles

WORLD EMPIRES OF BRITAIN, FRANCE, AND GERMANY 1914

KEY

- ◼ British Empire in 1914 (total population: 400,000,000).
- ▦ French Empire in 1914 (total population: 95,638,000).
- ▨ German Empire in 1914 (total population: 68,745,000).

Note: by the end of 1914, the only German overseas possession remaining uncaptured by the Allies was German East Africa.

Empire troops played a large part in the war, notably those of Britain.

© Arthur Banks 1973

THE FIRST BALKAN WAR 1912-1913*

❶ The General Situation

*Note: in two parts, viz.,
1. 18 Oct. - 3 Dec. 1912.
2. 3 Feb. - 10 May 1913.

Austria opposes Serbia's demand for a port on Adriatic coast

Russia supports Serbia's demand for a port on the Adriatic coast.

Rumania does not join Balkan allies but is keen to share in their gains.

Bulgaria is anxious to obtain territory to her south, most of which has been promised to her.

Greece occupies and wishes to retain Salonika, which is claimed by Bulgaria.

AUSTRIA-HUNGARY
RUMANIA
Belgrade
Bucharest
SERBIA
Black Sea
BULGARIA
Sofia
Adriatic Sea
Scutari
Midia
MONTE-NEGRO
ITALY
OTTOMAN TURKEY EMPIRE
Adrianople
Constantinople
Salonika
Enos

KEY
▨ Countries of the Balkan League.
▧ Territory lost by Turkey at Peace of London.

0 — 200
Miles

Aegean Sea

Montenegro declared war on Turkey on 8 October 1912, and the other three Christian states presented their ultimatums to Turkey on 18 October whereupon Turkey replied by declaring war upon them. Britain and Germany restrained their allies temporarily to avoid a full-scale conflict enveloping Europe, but Turkey lost territory.

MAIN REASON FOR WAR: BALKAN STATES EAGER TO "LIBERATE" THEIR COMPATRIOTS STILL WITHIN TURKEY IN EUROPE.

❷ The Military Operations

RUMANIA

KEY
▷▷▷ Montenegrin advances.
▷▷ Serb advances.
▨▷ Greek advances.
≫≫ Bulgar advances.
◀ Turkish counter-attacks.

SERBIA
Drina
Lim
Ibar
Danube
Niš
Iskûr
BOSNIA
Cetinje
Sofia
BULGARIA
Tunje
Yambol
Burgas
Black Sea
FALLS
MONTE-NEGRO
Scutari
Kustendil
Skoplje
Kumanovo
Plovdiv
Kirk Kilisse
Armistice concluded.
Durazzo
Vardar
Adrianople
FALLS 25/3/13
Maritsa
Lule Burgas
Midia
Tirana
Monastir
EMPIRE
Chatalja
Adriatic Sea
OTTOMAN
(TURKEY)
Constantinople
Aliakmon
Salonika
Enos
Gallipoli
Grevena
FALLS 6/3/13
Janina
Larissa
0 — 50
Miles
GREECE
Preveza
© Arthur Banks 1973

The Serbs gained victories at Kumanovo (23 October) and Monastir (15 November). The Bulgarians gained victories at Kirk Kilisse (23 October) and Lule Burgas (30 October), but failed in their attack on the fortified lines of Chatalja (17-18 November). The Greeks moved into Macedonia occupying Salonika on 9 November.

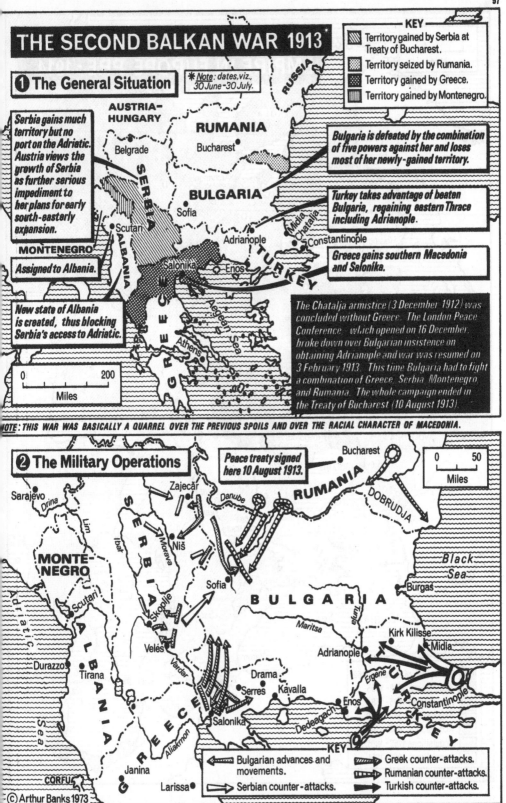

THE SECOND BALKAN WAR 1913 *

KEY
- Territory gained by Serbia at Treaty of Bucharest.
- Territory seized by Rumania.
- Territory gained by Greece.
- Territory gained by Montenegro.

❶ The General Situation

Note: dates, viz. 30 June – 30 July.

Serbia gains much territory but no port on the Adriatic. Austria views the growth of Serbia as further serious impediment to her plans for early south-easterly expansion.

MONTENEGRO

Assigned to Albania.

New state of Albania is created, thus blocking Serbia's access to Adriatic.

Bulgaria is defeated by the combination of five powers against her and loses most of her newly-gained territory.

Turkey takes advantage of beaten Bulgaria, regaining eastern Thrace including Adrianople.

Greece gains southern Macedonia and Salonika.

The Chatalja armistice (3 December 1912) was concluded without Greece. The London Peace Conference, which opened on 16 December, broke down over Bulgarian insistence on obtaining Adrianople and war was resumed on 3 February 1913. This time Bulgaria had to fight a combination of Greece, Serbia, Montenegro, and Rumania. The whole campaign ended in the Treaty of Bucharest (10 August 1913).

AUSTRIA–HUNGARY · RUMANIA · Bucharest · Belgrade · SERBIA · BULGARIA · Sofia · Scutari · ALBANIA · Adrianople · Midia · Chatalia · Constantinople · Salonika · Enos · TURKEY · GREECE · Aegean Sea · Athens · RUSSIA

0 — 200 Miles

NOTE: THIS WAR WAS BASICALLY A QUARREL OVER THE PREVIOUS SPOILS AND OVER THE RACIAL CHARACTER OF MACEDONIA.

❷ The Military Operations

Peace treaty signed here 10 August 1913.

0 — 50 Miles

Bucharest · Zajecǎr · Danube · RUMANIA · DOBRUDJA · Sarajevo · Drina · SERBIA · Ibar · Morava · Niš · Lim · MONTENEGRO · Sofia · BULGARIA · Black Sea · Burgas · Scutari · Skoplje · Maritsa · Velés · Vardar · Drama · Adrianople · Kirk Kilisse · Midia · ALBANIA · Durazzo · Tirana · Serres · Kavalla · Ergene · Enos · Constantinople · Salonika · Dedeagach · TURKEY · GREECE · Aliakmon · Janina · CORFU · Larissa · Adriatic Sea

KEY
- ⟸ Bulgarian advances and movements.
- ⟹ Serbian counter-attacks.
- ⟹ Greek counter-attacks.
- ⟹ Rumanian counter-attacks.
- ➤ Turkish counter-attacks.

© Arthur Banks 1973

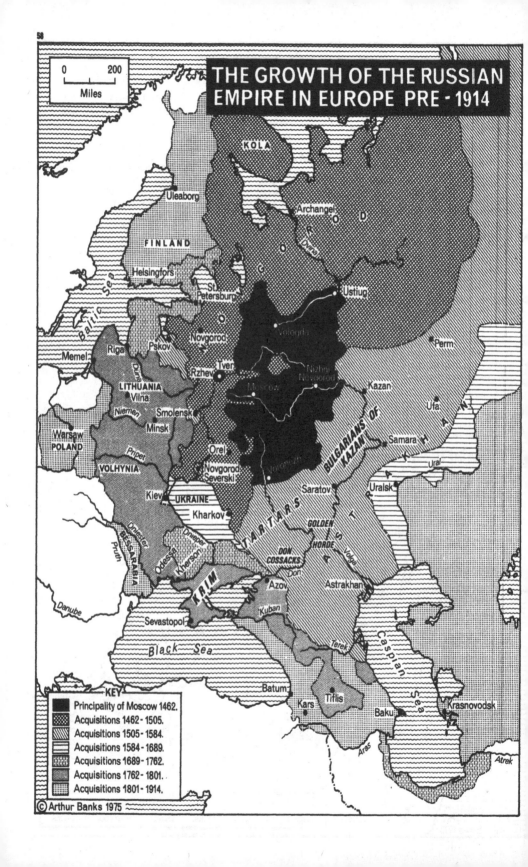

58

THE GROWTH OF THE RUSSIAN EMPIRE IN EUROPE PRE - 1914

KEY

- Principality of Moscow 1462.
- Acquisitions 1462 - 1505.
- Acquisitions 1505 - 1584.
- Acquisitions 1584 - 1689.
- Acquisitions 1689 - 1762.
- Acquisitions 1762 - 1801.
- Acquisitions 1801 - 1914.

© Arthur Banks 1975

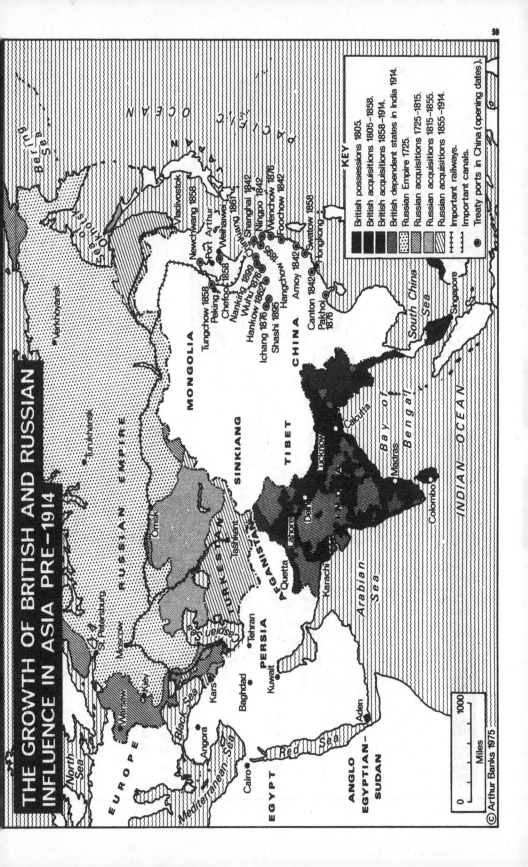

THE MIDDLE EAST PRE–1914

Russian Zone (1907 onwards).

British Zone (1907 onwards).

Neutral Zone (1907 onwards).

800

0

Miles

CHINA

INDIA

Bombay

TURKESTAN

Tashkent

Samarkand

Merv

AFGHANISTAN

Herat

Kabul

Indus

BALUCHISTAN

Karachi

Aral Sea

RUSSIA

PERSIA

Caspian Sea

Meshed

Tehran

Isfahan

Muscat

OMAN

ARABIAN

GULF

Batum

Tigris

Euphrates

Persian Gulf

QATAR

N E J D

HADRAMAUT

FRENCH SOMALILAND

BRITISH SOMALILAND

ITALIAN SOMALILAND

Constantinople

Smyrna

Aleppo

Damascus

Jerusalem

OTTOMAN EMPIRE

HEJAZ

Medina

Jiddah

Mecca

Red Sea

ASSIR

YEMEN

Hodeida

Aden

ERITREA

ABYSSINIA

Mediterranean Sea

Cairo

Nile

EGYPT

ANGLO-EGYPTIAN SUDAN

© Arthur Banks 1975

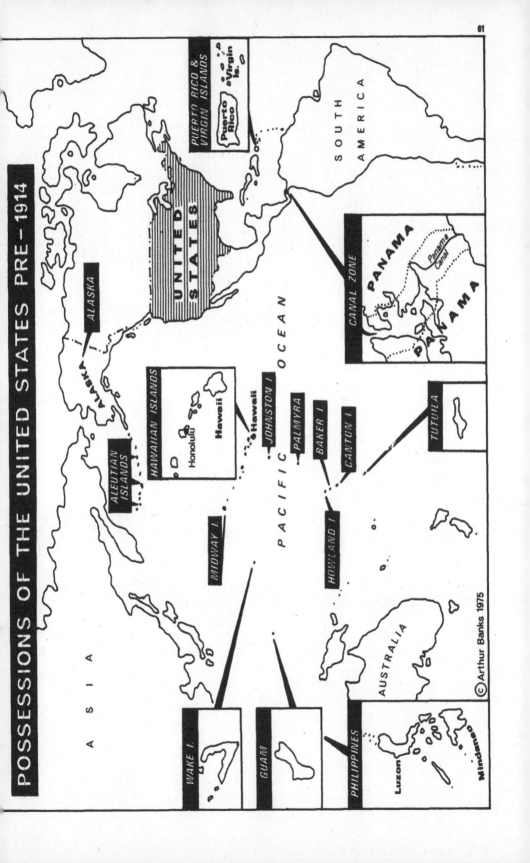

POSSESSIONS OF THE UNITED STATES PRE – 1914

61

PUERTO RICO &
VIRGIN ISLANDS

Puerto
Rico

Virgin
is.

SOUTH
AMERICA

UNITED
STATES

ALASKA

ALASKA I

ALEUTIAN
ISLANDS

CANAL ZONE

PANAMA

Panama
Canal

PANAMA

PACIFIC OCEAN

HAWAIIAN ISLANDS

Honolulu

Hawaii

Hawaii

JOHNSTON I

PALMYRA

BAKER I

CANTON I

TUTUILA

MIDWAY I

HOWLAND I

ASIA

AUSTRALIA

WAKE I.

GUAM

PHILIPPINES

Luzon

Mindanao

© Arthur Banks 1975

IV
THE FIRST WORLD WAR

64

EUROPE IN 1914

Note the extents of Germany and Austria-Hungary.

© Arthur Banks 1975

0   400
Miles

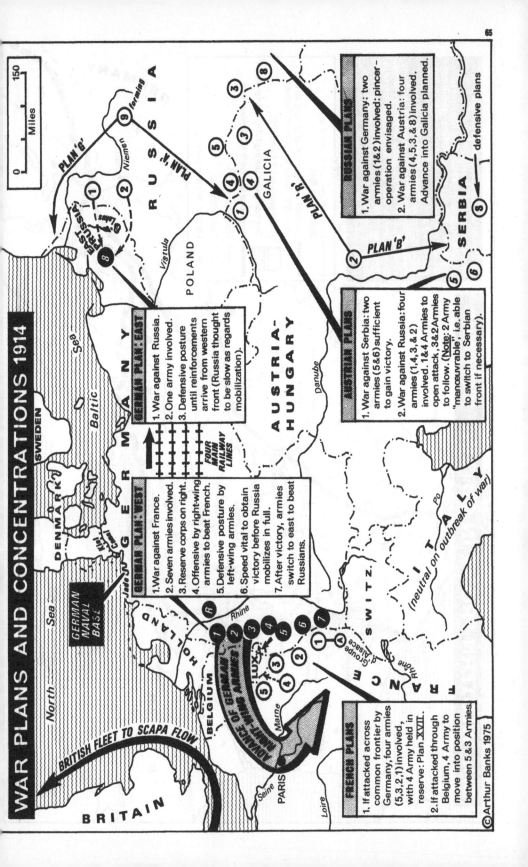

WAR PLANS AND CONCENTRATIONS 1914

BRITISH FLEET TO SCAPA FLOW

GERMAN NAVAL BASE

GERMAN PLAN WEST

1. War against France.
2. Seven armies involved.
3. Reserve corps on right.
4. Offensive by right-wing armies to beat French.
5. Defensive posture by left-wing armies.
6. Speed vital to obtain victory before Russia mobilizes in full.
7. After victory, armies switch to east to beat Russians.

GERMAN PLAN EAST

1. War against Russia.
2. One army involved.
3. Defensive posture until reinforcements arrive from western front (Russia thought to be slow as regards mobilization).

FOUR MAIN RAILWAY LINES

FRENCH PLANS

1. If attacked across common frontier by Germany, four armies (5,3,2,1) involved, with 4 Army held in reserve: Plan XVII.
2. If attacked through Belgium, 4 Army to move into position between 5 & 3 Armies.

AUSTRIAN PLANS

1. War against Serbia: two armies (5&6) sufficient to gain victory.
2. War against Russia: four armies (1,4,3, & 2) involved. 1&4 Armies to open attack, 3&2 Armies to follow. (Note: 2 Army "manœuvrable", i.e. able to switch to Serbian front if necessary).

RUSSIAN PLANS

1. War against Germany: two armies (1&2) involved: pincer-operation envisaged.
2. War against Austria: four armies (4,5,3, & 8) involved. Advance into Galicia planned.

← defensive plans

PLAN 'G'

PLAN 'R'

PLAN 'R'

PLAN 'B'

© Arthur Banks 1975

THE WESTERN FRONT IN OUTLINE 1914 – 1918

The campaign was really one prolonged battle involving territorial gains and losses completely disproportionate to the casualties involved. The basic stages were: the initial German advance of 1914 which was halted at the Marne and Aisne battles: the resulting 'race to the sea' (a series of outflanking moves): the fairly stabilized trench line being established: the Allied gains and fights at the Somme and Verdun: the German offensives in the spring of 1918: the Allied advance towards Germany that halted with the Armistice on 11 November 1918

KEY

.... Limit of German advance in September 1914.

▬ ▬ ▬ General front from end of 1914 to 30 June 1916 (prior to Somme battles).

▓▓ Allied gains in 1916 and 1917.

▨▨ German gains during 1918 offensives.

▬▬ Armistice line on 11 November 1918.

—·—·— Frontiers in 1914.

● Capital cities.

• ∘ Other cities and towns.

GERMANY

LORRAINE

Lunéville

Metz

Nancy

Moselle

Meuse

St. Mihiel

Verdun

Longwy

Liège

Namur

Meuse

Louvain

Antwerp

BRUSSELS

Charleroi

Sambre

Schelde

Ghent

Bruges

Zeebrugge

Ostend

Nieuport

Dunkirk

Calais

Boulogne

Dieppe

NORTH SEA

Strait of Dover

HOLLAND

Dixmude

Ypres

Messines

Givenchy

Neuve Chapelle

La Bassée

Lille

Courtrai

Tournai

Lys

Mons

Valenciennes

Maubeuge

Landrecies

Le Cateau

Cambrai

Douai

Lens

Vimy

Arras

Albert

Péronne

Bapaume

Quéant

St. Quentin

Oise

La Fère

Laon

Noyon

Montdidier

Amiens

Somme

Compiègne

Oise

Meaux

PARIS

Seine

Mézières

Sedan

Aisne

Soissons

CHEMIN DES DAMES

Vesle

Rheims

Épernay

Château-Thierry

Marne

Petit Morin

Grand Morin

Aisne

Marne

Rouen

LUXEMBURG

BELGIQUE

FRANCE

CHAMPAGNE

0	30

Miles

© Arthur Banks 1973

THE EASTERN FRONT IN OUTLINE
1914 - 1918

The battle fronts were not continuous and therefore, the lines on map are generalized. The trench system was not so detailed as on the Western Front and the limits of advances or retreats were not contemporaneous. For example, the Russian advance into East Prussia in 1914 was ended at Tannenberg before their large gains in Galicia were achieved.

KEY
- — ·— Frontiers in 1914.
- ● Capital cities.
- ● Other cities and towns.

0   200

Miles

Gulf of Finland

Revel

ST. PETERSBURG
(Petrograd)

Narva

Baltic Sea

Gulf of Riga

Pskov

Riga

Libau

Dvinsk

Memel

Dvina

Moscow

Königsberg

Kovno

Danzig

Vilna

Smolensk

EAST PRUSSIA

Tannenberg

Masuria

Grodno

Minsk

Narew

Niemen

Vistula

Prasnysz

R   U   S   S   I   A

Warsaw

Brest-Litovsk

Pinsk

Pripet

P O L A N D

Desna

Lodz

Pripet Marshes

Radom

Lublin

Lutsk

Rovno

Kiev

Cracow

Lemberg

Brody

Vorskla

Jaroslav

G A L I C I A

Przemysl

Tarnopol

San

Dnieper

Carpathian Mountains

Stanislau

AUSTRIA - Mountains

Dniester

Bug

Nikolaiev

Budapest

Czernovitz

BUKOVINA

HUNGARY

Prath

Kishinev

MOLDAVIA

Odessa

Drava

Danube

Tisza

TRANSYLVANIA

BESS-ARABIA

Sava

R   U   M   A   N   I   A

BELGRADE

WALLACHIA

BUCHAREST

DOBRUDJA

MONTE-NEGRO

SERBIA

Danube

BULGARIA

KEY
- ▬ ▬ ▬ Limit of Russian advances 1914 - 1915.
- ••••••• Limit of German advances 1915 - 1916.
- ▨ Territory regained by Brusilov, June - August 1916.
- ▧ German gains in September 1917.
- ▬▬▬ Extent of German penetration into Russia by 3 March 1918 (Treaty of Brest-Litovsk).

© Arthur Banks 1973

OPENING MOVES INVOLVING GERMANY

1 — PLAN — NETH. BEL. LUX. **GERMANY** *major ATTACKS minor* DEFENSIVE RUSSIA • Paris FRANCE AUSTRIA-HUNGARY

2 — BRITAIN NETH. BEL. **GERMANY** RAPID MOBILISATION RUSSIA AID FRANCE APPEAL FOR DIVERSIONARY ACTION AUSTRIA-HUNGARY

3 — Antwerp ★ DELAY NETH. **BELGIUM** **GERMANY** FRANCE Maubeuge ★ DELAY Liège ★ DELAY Namur DELAY FIRST ARMY to Paris DIVERGING SECOND ARMY LUX. FRANCE

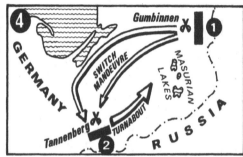

4 — Gumbinnen **GERMANY** SWITCH MANOEUVRE MASURIAN LAKES Tannenberg TURNABOUT RUSSIA

5 — **GERMANY** TWO CORPS SWITCH FRONTS (BY RAIL) WEAKENED • Paris STRENGTHENED RUSSIA AUSTRIA-HUNGARY

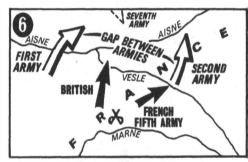

6 — SEVENTH ARMY AISNE AISNE GAP BETWEEN ARMIES FIRST ARMY SECOND ARMY BRITISH VESLE FRANCE FRENCH FIFTH ARMY MARNE

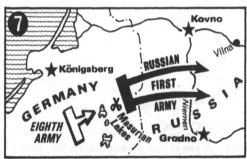

7 — Kovno ★ Vilna • RUSSIAN ★ Königsberg FIRST **GERMANY** ARMY RUSSIA EIGHTH ARMY Masurian Lakes Niemen Grodno ★

8 — Lys **BELGIUM** Belgians B.E.F. FRANCE LUX. FRENCH Somme Oise AISNE

© Arthur Banks 1975

These sections depict basic military moves involving Germany in the first weeks of the European campaign and illustrate how events and situations on her western and eastern fronts affected and reacted upon each other. In brief, her overall effort was split and she rapidly became involved in an active two-front war situation, the very position for which her detailed pre-war plans had been designed to avoid. These moves are shown in more detail on following pages.

OPENING MOVES INVOLVING OTHER POWERS

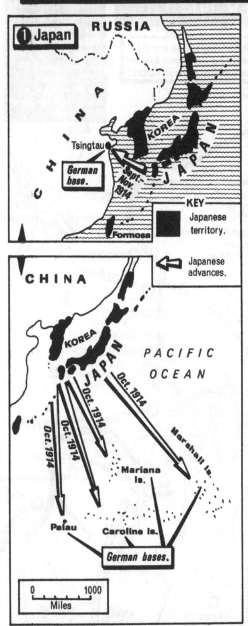

① Japan

RUSSIA

CHINA

KOREA

JAPAN

Tsingtau

German base.

Sept.–Nov. 1914

Formosa

KEY

Japanese territory.

Japanese advances.

CHINA

KOREA

JAPAN

PACIFIC OCEAN

Oct. 1914

Oct. 1914

Oct. 1914

Oct. 1914

Marshall Is.

Mariana Is.

Palau

Caroline Is.

German bases.

0   1000
Miles

② Austria-Hungary

RUSSIA

GERMANY

Russians

AUSTRIA-HUNGARY

SWITZ.

ITALY

MONTENEGRO

SERBIA

ALB.

RUMANIA

BULGARIA

GREECE

KEY
Austrian attacks.

③ France

BELGIUM

Ardennes

LUX.

GERMANY

FRANCE

Metz

Aug. 1914

Aug. 1914

Toul

Aug. 1914

Epinal

Aug. 1914

Belfort

KEY
French attacks.

0   500
Miles

© Arthur Banks 1975

These sections depict basic moves involving Japan, Austria-Hungary, and France during the opening months of the war. In the Far East, Japan attacked and captured the German mainland base at Tsingtau plus a number of German Pacific islands. In Europe, Austria-Hungary met with rebuffs in clashes with Russia and Serbia. France attempted operations against Germany, but these moves came to naught. Consequently, with Russia and Britain involved also, the conflict rapidly engulfed hundreds of millions of people.

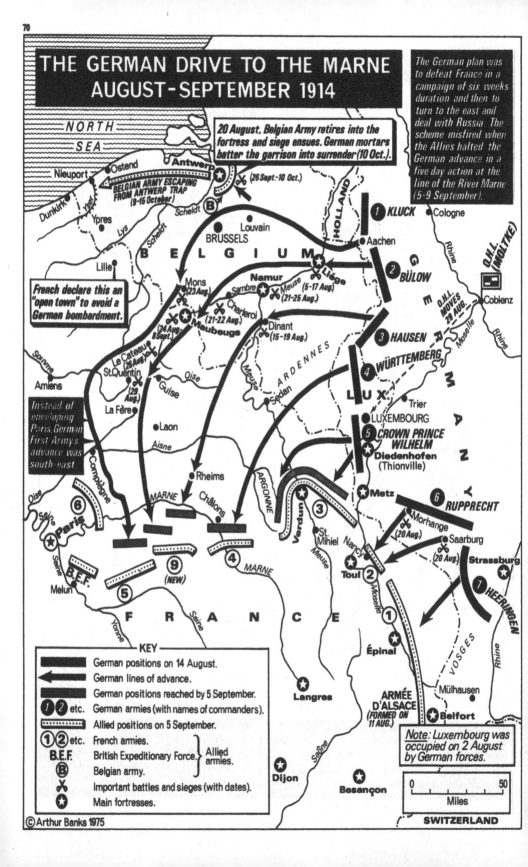

THE GERMAN DRIVE TO THE MARNE
AUGUST-SEPTEMBER 1914

The German plan was to defeat France in a campaign of six weeks duration and then to turn to the east and deal with Russia. The scheme misfired when the Allies halted the German advance in a five day action at the line of the River Marne (5-9 September).

NORTH SEA

20 August, Belgian Army retires into the fortress and siege ensues. German mortars batter the garrison into surrender (10 Oct.).

Nieuport • Ostend

Antwerp (26 Sept.-10 Oct.)

BELGIAN ARMY ESCAPING FROM ANTWERP TRAP (9-15 October)

Dunkirk • Yser • Ypres • Lille

B E L G I U M

HOLLAND

1 KLUCK • Cologne

Louvain
BRUSSELS

Aachen

2 BÜLOW

O.H.L. (MOLTKE)

Rhine

Lys • Scheldt

French declare this an "open town" to avoid a German bombardment.

Mons (23 Aug.) • Namur • Liège (5-17 Aug.)
Sambre • Meuse (21-25 Aug.)

Charleroi (21-22 Aug.)

Maubeuge (24 Aug.-8 Sept.)

Dinant (15-19 Aug.)

O.H.L. MOVES 29 Aug.

Coblenz

3 HAUSEN

4 WÜRTTEMBERG

Moselle

Le Cateau (26 Aug.)
St.Quentin (29 Aug.)
La Fère

Oise • Guise

A R D E N N E S

Sedan

L U X

Trier

G E R M A N Y

Amiens

Instead of enveloping Paris, German First Army's advance was south-east.

• Laon

Aisne

Meuse

LUXEMBOURG

5 CROWN PRINCE WILHELM

Diedenhofen (Thionville)

Rhine

Somme

Compiègne

• Rheims

Châlons

MARNE

A R G O N N E

Verdun

Metz

6 RUPPRECHT

Morhange (20 Aug.)

Saarburg (20 Aug.)

Strassburg

Oise

6
Paris
Seine

B.E.F.

Melun

5

9 (NEW)

4

MARNE

3

St. Mihiel

Nancy

Toul **2**

1

7 HEERINGEN

F R A N C E

Yonne • Seine

Meuse • Moselle

Épinal

V O S G E S

Rhine

Langres

ARMÉE D'ALSACE (FORMED ON 11 AUG.)

Mülhausen

Note: Luxembourg was occupied on 2 August by German forces.

KEY

▬▬	German positions on 14 August.
◀━	German lines of advance.
▬	German positions reached by 5 September.
①② etc.	German armies (with names of commanders).
··········	Allied positions on 5 September.
①② etc.	French armies.
B.E.F.	British Expeditionary Force. } Allied armies.
B	Belgian army.
✗	Important battles and sieges (with dates).
✪	Main fortresses.

• Dijon

• Besançon

0 — 50
Miles

© Arthur Banks 1975

SWITZERLAND

• Belfort

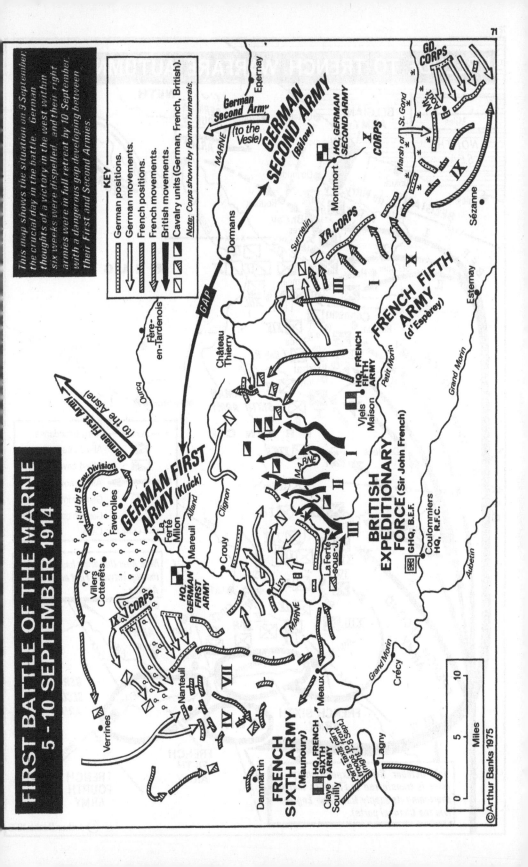

FIRST BATTLE OF THE MARNE 5 - 10 SEPTEMBER 1914

This map shows the situation on 9 September, the crucial day in the battle. German thoughts of a victory in the west within six weeks were dispelled, and their right armies were in full retreat by 10 September with a dangerous gap developing between their First and Second Armies.

KEY

- ⬛ German positions.
- ⬜ German movements.
- ▨ French positions.
- ▧ French movements.
- ⬛ British movements.
- Cavalry units (German, French, British).

Note: Corps shown by Roman numerals.

GD. CORPS

German Second Army (to the Vesle)

Epernay

GERMAN SECOND ARMY (Bülow)

MARNE

Dormans

HQ, GERMAN SECOND ARMY

X CORPS

Mt. Toil

Marsh of St. Gond

IX

Sézanne

Montmort

XR. CORPS

III

I

X

FRENCH FIFTH ARMY (d'Espèrey)

Esternay

Surmelin

GAP

Fère-en-Tardenois

Château Thierry

HQ, FRENCH FIFTH ARMY

Viels Maison

I

Petit Morin

Grand Morin

Ourcq

German First Army (to the Aisne)

laid by 5 Cav.Division

Villers Cotterêts

Faverolles

GERMAN FIRST ARMY (Kluck)

La Ferté Milon

Mareuil

Alland

Crouy

Clignon

MARNE

II

III

La Ferté sous-J.

I

BRITISH EXPEDITIONARY FORCE (Sir John French)

GHQ, B.E.F.

Coulommiers

HQ, R.F.C.

Grand Morin

Aubetin

IX CORPS

HQ, GERMAN FIRST ARMY

Lizy

Lizy

MARNE

Nanteuil

VII

Meaux

Crécy

Verrines

IV

Dammartin

FRENCH SIXTH ARMY (Maunoury)

HQ, FRENCH SIXTH ARMY

Claye Souilly

Paris taxis carry troops 7-8 Sept.

Paris (to 8 Sept.)

Lagny

Miles

0 — 5 — 10

© Arthur Banks 1975

PRELUDE TO TRENCH WARFARE AUTUMN 1914

0 20
Miles

NORTH SEA

NETH.

GERMAN FOURTH ARMY

Antwerp

BELGIAN ARMY

BESELER 'GROUP'

Ostend
Bruges
Ghent

Nieuport
Dixmude
Roulers
Ypres
Messines

BELGIANS

Dunkirk
Calais

de Mitry
Fr.Terr.
Br.Cav.

B.E.F. I

III

St.Omer
Hazebrouck
Armentières
LILLE

II
Lys

Conneau
Béthune
La Bassée
Lens

XXI
d'Urbal
Vimy

St.Pol

Arras
X G

FRANCE

GERMAN SIXTH ARMY

Mons
Charleroi
Sambre

Maubeuge

BELGIUM

BRUSSELS

Schelde
Lys
Escaut

I Bav. R.
Scarpe
IV

Doullens

XI
XIV R
II Bav.

Somme
I Bav.
XX

AMIENS
Chaulnes

XVIII
Poix

XIV
IV
II

XIII
Roye
IX R
IV R
IX

Compiegne

Soissons

FRENCH SIXTH ARMY

B.E.F.

FRENCH FIFTH ARMY

KEY

──xxxx──	Army boundaries.
⊠	Allied infantry corps.
◨	Allied cavalry corps.
➡	Allied moves.
⊠	German infantry corps.
◨	German cavalry corps.
··········	Canal.

Note how this army has plugged the gap between First and Second Armies.

GERMAN SEVENTH ARMY

La Fère
Oise
Laon
Craonne
Vailly
Aisne

GERMAN FIRST ARMY

III

RHEIMS

GERMAN SECOND ARMY

GERMAN FOURTH ARMY...

5-15 October, British Expeditionary Force is transferred to Flanders thereby shortening its supply link from England (via the Channel ports).

© Arthur Banks 1975

BATTLE OF THE YSER
18-31 OCTOBER 1914

21 October, French lay mines off Ostend to protect flotilla against emerging U-boats.

The German objectives were the Channel ports to sever the Allied sea link with England, but the Belgians stemmed the advance by opening the Nieuport sluices to admit the North Sea. An artificial lake was created by this manoeuvre.

KEY

0 1 2 3 4 5 Miles

Railways.
Canals.
Forest.

Note: this map has been extended to Ypres to convey the situation on the Belgian right flank.

Commencing 18 October, Allied naval flotilla (including British monitors) bombards German batteries shelling Nieuport.

OSTEND

GERMAN ADVANCE FROM ANTWERP

GERMAN (Württemberg) FOURTH ARMY

Middelkerke
4 Ersatz Div.
Leffinghe
Ghistelles
Westende
Lombartzyde
NORTH SEA
Slype
III RESERVE CORPS
SAND DUNES 2 Div.
Mannekensvere
5 Reserve Div.
NIEUPORT
St. Georges
Schoore
1 Div.
Coxyde
Ramscapelle
6 Reserve Div.
Couckelaere
Schoorbakke
BELGIAN 3 Div.
Tervaete
Keyem
Thourout
2 Cavalry Div.
ARMY
to Dunkirk and Calais
Avecapelle
Pervyse
4 Div.
Marine Fusiliers
43 Reserve Div.
XXII RESERVE CORPS
44 Reserve Div.
FURNES

26 October, Belgians dam culverts beneath railway embankment.

5 Div.
Dixmude
Zarren
Cortemarck
1 Brigade (3 Div.)
Clercken
Woumen
1 Cav.Div.
DE MITRY'S CAVALRY CORPS
45 Res. Div.
XXIII RES. CORPS
46 Res. Div.
ROULERS
Loo
Yser
Fort of Knokke
FOREST OF HOUTHULST
Staden
51 Res. Div.
R. CORPS
89 Territorial Div.
Merckem
Westroosebeke
52 Res. Div.
XXVII R. CORPS
6 Div.
Bixschoote
Poelcapelle
3 Cav.Div.
Historical note: in 1600, Maurice of Nassau, after his victory near Nieuport, had to lift his siege of the town when the defenders opened sluices to flood area.
Steenstraat
Langemarck
Passchendaele
53 Res. Div.
Boesinghe
Pilckem
BRITISH IV CORPS
XXVII RES. CORPS
7 Div.
54 Res. Div.
Wieltje

MILITARY KEY
THE GENERAL POSITION 18 OCTOBER
German attacks (division strength).
Belgian infantry. — Belgian cavalry.
French infantry. — French cavalry.
British infantry. — British cavalry.
Area flooded by Belgians 28-30 October.

87 Territorial Div.
YPRES

© Arthur Banks 1975

THE TANNENBERG CAMPAIGN 20–31 AUGUST 1914

KEY

☐ German corps plus one division (20 August).
■ Russian corps (20 August).
⇓ German 'switch' moves (21–29 August).
↓ Russian movements (to 31 August).
◨ German cavalry division (22–31 August).
▨ Area where Russians capitulated.
★ German fortresses.
┼┼┼ Railways.

Note: sole German division confronting Russian First Army (unaware of the situation).

FIRST ARMY (Rennenkampf)

GAP BETWEEN RUSSIAN ARMIES

JILINSKY
ARMY GROUP
RUSSIA

SECOND ARMY (Samsonov)

FORTIFIED ZONE

MASURIAN LAKES

Gumbinnen
Insterburg
Königsberg
Angerburg
Lötzen
Allenstein
Tannenberg
Soldau
Deutsch Eylau
Elbing
Marienburg
Graudenz
Vistula
Thorn

slow advance
by rail
marching
by rail

© Arthur Banks 1975

0   20
Miles

74

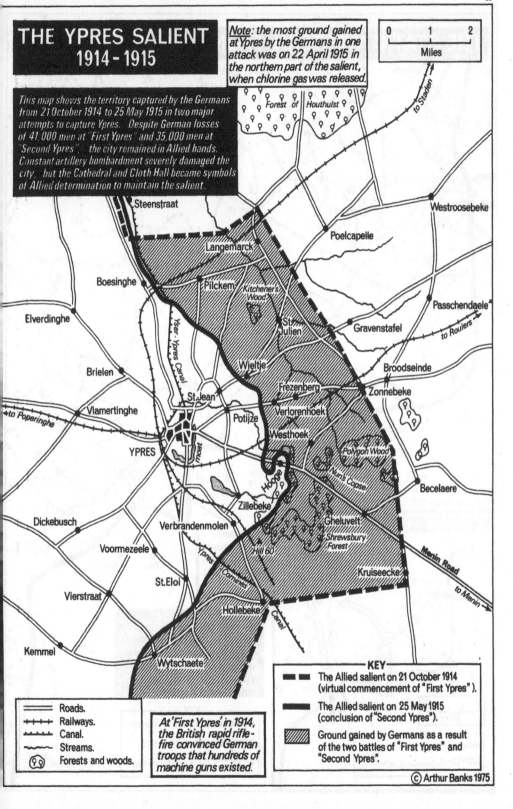

THE YPRES SALIENT
1914-1915

<u>Note</u>: the most ground gained at Ypres by the Germans in one attack was on 22 April 1915 in the northern part of the salient, when chlorine gas was released.

0   1   2
Miles

This map shows the territory captured by the Germans from 21 October 1914 to 25 May 1915 in two major attempts to capture Ypres. Despite German losses of 41,000 men at "First Ypres" and 35,000 men at "Second Ypres", the city remained in Allied hands. Constant artillery bombardment severely damaged the city, but the Cathedral and Cloth Hall became symbols of Allied determination to maintain the salient.

Forest of Houthulst
Steenstraat
Westroosebeke
Langemarck
Poelcapelle
Boesinghe
Pilckem
Kitcheners Wood
Passchendaele
Elverdinghe
St. Julien
Gravenstafel
to Roulers
Brielen
Wieltje
Broodseinde
Yser-Ypres Canal
Frezenberg
Zonnebeke
Vlamertinghe
St.Jean
Verlorenhoek
to Poperinghe
Potijze
Westhoek
Polygon Wood
YPRES
Nun's Copse
Becelaere
Hooge
Zillebeke
Menin Road
Dickebusch
Verbrandenmolen
Gheluvelt
Shrewsbury Forest
Voormezeele
Hill 60
Kruiseecke
St.Eloi
to Menin
Vierstraat
Hollebeke
Kemmel
Wytschaete

KEY
- The Allied salient on 21 October 1914 (virtual commencement of "First Ypres").
- The Allied salient on 25 May 1915 (conclusion of "Second Ypres").
- Ground gained by Germans as a result of the two battles of "First Ypres" and "Second Ypres".

Roads. Railways. Canal. Streams. Forests and woods.

At 'First Ypres' in 1914, the British rapid rifle-fire convinced German troops that hundreds of machine guns existed.

© Arthur Banks 1975

THE STATIC WESTERN FRONT 1915

0   40
Miles

Bruges

Antwerp

Düsseldorf

Ghent

Ypres

BRUSSELS

Cologne

Lille

Bonn

N.Chapelle

Liége

Festubert

B E L G I U M

G

Loos

Lens

Mons

Namur

Douai

Arras

A R T O I S

Cambrai

ARDENNES

Péronne

LUXEMBOURG

St.Quentin

Hirson

E
R
M

Mézières

Noyon

Sedan

A

Laon

N

Compiègne

Soissons

Perthes

Verdun

Rheims

C
H
A
M
P
A
G
N
E

A
R
G
O
N
N
E

Metz

© Arthur Banks 1973

Châlons

St.
Mihiel

L
O
R
R
A
I
N
E

JOFFRE'S PLANS IN EARLY 1915

BRUSSELS

Cologne

Rhine

Toul

Nancy

Lille

B E L G I U M

HOLL

G

Douai

trench

Hirson

Mézières

F

Noyon

R
A
N
C
E

U
X

E
R
M
A
N
Y

**THIS GERMAN
SALIENT EXISTED
(WITH VARIATIONS)
UNTIL SEPTEMBER
1918.**

Épinal

V
O
S
G
E
S

Rheims

warfare

Metz

St.Mihiel

0   60
Miles

Nancy

*Despite Allied efforts to achieve
a breakthrough, the basic shape
of the front line remained virtually
unaltered on small scale maps.
Note the important rail network
under German control.*

A
L
S
A
C
E

── KEY ──
➤ Opening attacks.
⇨ Subsequent advances.

── KEY ──
━━ Front line in February.
➤ Allied offensives.
⇦ German offensives.

Belfort

THE MOBILE EASTERN FRONT 1915

0   50   100
Miles

Riga

Libau
Fell on 8 May.

Not captured by Germans.

Memel

Dvinsk

Dvina

Stormed by Germans 17-18 August.

BALTIC SEA

Kovno

Germany's aim was to make the Eastern Front safe and passive so that she could switch her main assault to the Western Front (she did not hope to completely defeat Russia). Rather than instituting an enveloping operation, she decided to attempt a breakthrough attack between Gorlice and Tarnow. This commenced on 2 May 1915 in concert with the Austrians. This front contrasts sharply with the Western Front during 1915.

Königsberg

Danzig

EAST

PRUSSIA

MASURIAN LAKES

Vistula

Graudenz

Grodno

Niemen

Narew

RUSSIA

Thorn

Fell on 2 September.

Capitulated on 20 August.

Vistula

Entered by Germans on 5 August.

Novo-Georgievsk

Warsaw

Bug

Brest-Litovsk

North of this position, the front line remained as shown (with minor variations) until the end of 1917.

POLAND

Vistula

Surrendered on 26 August.

Pripet

Ivangorod

South of this position, the front line remained as shown (with minor variations) until June 1916.

Fell on 5 August.

San

Evacuated by Russians on 22 June.

Vistula

Tarnow

Lemberg

Cracow

G A L I C I A

2 MAY 1915

Przemysl

KEY

GERMAN ELEVENTH ARMY

Gorlice

Dniester

◇ Opening assault by German and Austrian armies.

▨ Advances by German and Austrian armies.

Fell on 3 June.

CARPATHIAN MOUNTAINS

Pruth

Tisza

······· Front line, 2 May.
——— Front line, 1 June.
▭▭▭ Front line, 16 July.
▱▱▱ Front line, 15 August.
– – – Front line, 1 September.
▲▲▲ Front line, winter 1915.

© Arthur Banks 1973

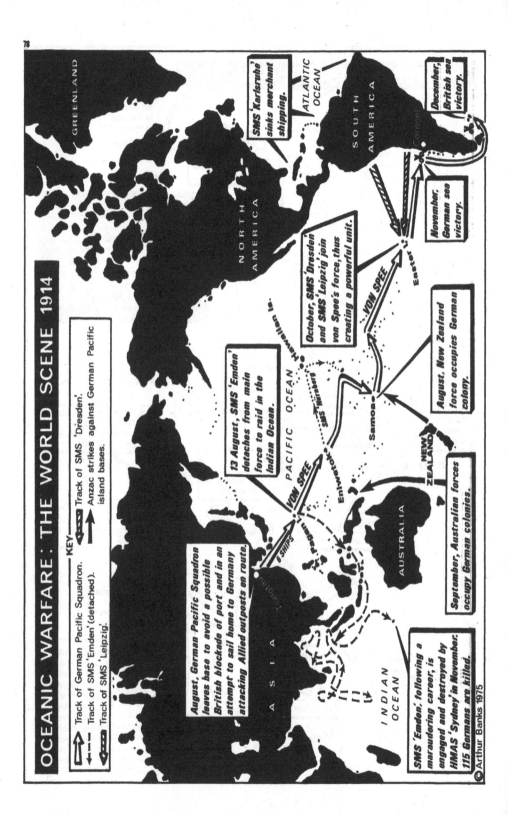

FIRST BATTLE OF THE ATLANTIC 1915-1918

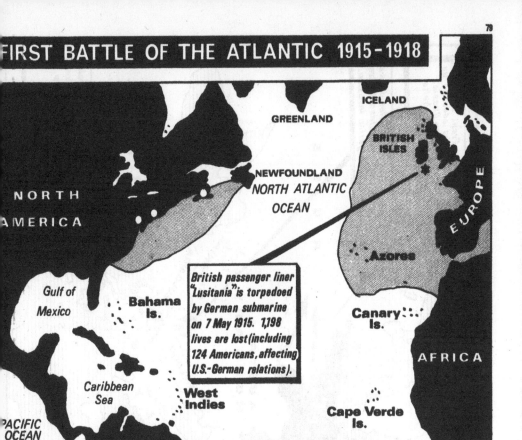

NORTH AMERICA
NORTH ATLANTIC OCEAN
GREENLAND
ICELAND
BRITISH ISLES
NEWFOUNDLAND
EUROPE
Azores
Gulf of Mexico
Bahama Is.
Canary Is.
AFRICA
Caribbean Sea
West Indies
Cape Verde Is.
PACIFIC OCEAN

British passenger liner "Lusitania" is torpedoed by German submarine on 7 May 1915. 1,198 lives are lost (including 124 Americans, affecting U.S.-German relations).

ALLIED CONVOY ROUTES

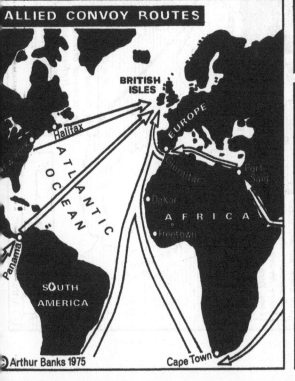

BRITISH ISLES
EUROPE
Halifax
ATLANTIC OCEAN
Gibraltar
Port Said
Dakar
AFRICA
Freetown
Panama
SOUTH AMERICA
Cape Town
© Arthur Banks 1975

KEY

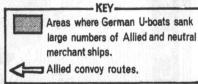

Areas where German U-boats sank large numbers of Allied and neutral merchant ships.

Allied convoy routes.

The heaviest German submarine assault on Allied merchant shipping was in 1917 when over two million tons was sunk. In May, the Allies introduced the convoy system (see below) which gradually reduced their losses.

destroyer (on zigzag course)
armed merchant ships
CONVOY COMMANDER (cruiser)
troop or merchant ships
scouting ship
armed merchant ships
destroyer (on zigzag course)

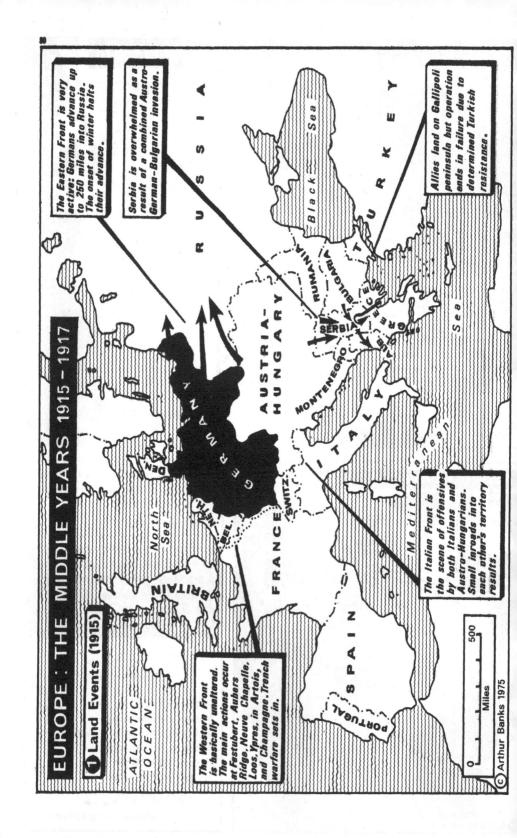

EUROPE: THE MIDDLE YEARS 1915-1917

①Land Events (1915)

The Eastern Front is very active: Germans advance up to 250 miles into Russia. The onset of winter halts their advance.

Serbia is overwhelmed as a result of a combined Austro-German-Bulgarian invasion.

Allies land on Gallipoli peninsula but operation ends in failure due to determined Turkish resistance.

The Western Front is basically unaltered. The main actions occur at Festubert, Aubers Ridge, Neuve Chapelle, Loos, Ypres, in Artois, and Champagne. Trench warfare sets in.

The Italian Front is the scene of offensives by both Italians and Austro-Hungarians. Small inroads into each other's territory results.

ATLANTIC OCEAN

North Sea

BRITAIN

DEN.

NETH.

BEL.

GERMANY

FRANCE

SWITZ.

SPAIN

PORTUGAL

Mediterranean Sea

ITALY

SWITZ.

AUSTRIA-HUNGARY

MONTENEGRO

SERBIA

RUMANIA

BULGARIA

GREECE

RUSSIA

Black Sea

TURKEY

0   500
Miles

© Arthur Banks 1975

EUROPE: THE MIDDLE YEARS 1915-1917

② Land Events (1916)

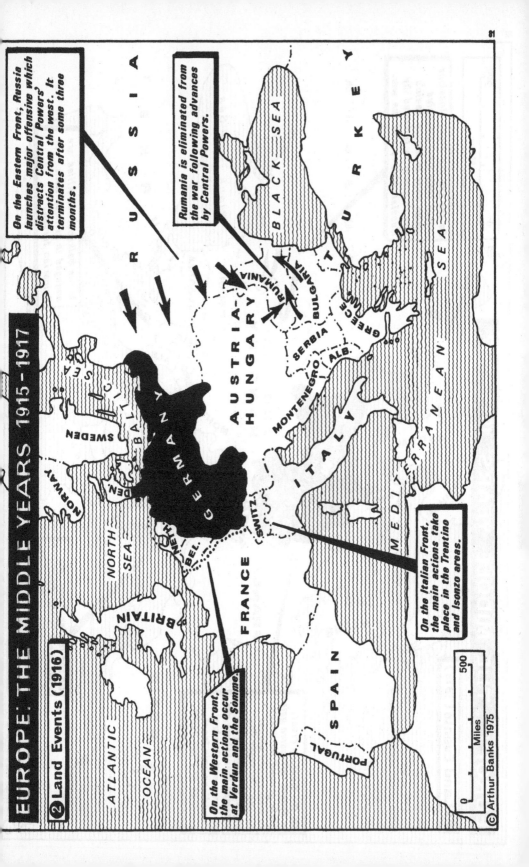

On the Eastern Front, Russia launches major offensive which distracts Central Powers' attention from the west. It terminates after some three months.

Rumania is eliminated from the war following advances by Central Powers.

On the Italian Front, the main actions take place in the Trentino and Isonzo areas.

On the Western Front, the main actions occur at Verdun and the Somme.

RUSSIA

SWEDEN

NORWAY

DEN.

BALTIC SEA

NORTH SEA

BRITAIN

ATLANTIC OCEAN

GERMANY

NETH.

BEL.

FRANCE

SWITZ.

SPAIN

PORTUGAL

AUSTRIA-HUNGARY

ITALY

MEDITERRANEAN SEA

MONTENEGRO

SERBIA

ALB.

GREECE

BULGARIA

RUMANIA

BLACK SEA

TURKEY

0   500
Miles

© Arthur Banks 1975

EUROPE: THE MIDDLE YEARS 1915~1917

③ Land Events (1917)

On the Eastern Front, Russians launch their final offensive which ends in failure. Lenin's rise to power is followed by Russian bids to end the war.

In the Balkans, the Allies are engaged in clashes with Bulgarian forces.

On the Italian Front, the main event is the Austro-German attack at Caporetto which pushes Italians back to the River Piave.

On the Western Front, a French offensive gains little ground but leads to widespread unrest among the front line units. British forces attempt breakthroughs at Ypres and Cambrai. Canadians gain local success at Vimy Ridge.

RUSSIA

TURKEY

Black Sea

RUMANIA

BULGARIA

SERBIA

MONTENEGRO

ALB.

AUSTRIA-HUNGARY

GERMANY (short of food and goods)

SWITZ.

SWEDEN

NORWAY

DEN.

North Sea

BRITAIN

FRANCE

ITALY

Mediterranean Sea

SPAIN

PORT.

ATLANTIC OCEAN

0   500
Miles

© Arthur Banks 1975

EUROPE: THE MIDDLE YEARS 1915-1917

④ Naval Events (1915-1917)

1915, Allied fleet fails to force passage.

1915, bombarded by Turco-German warships.

1916, battle of Jutland.

1915, battle of Dogger Bank.

1917, destroyer clash.

1916, bombarded by German warships.

BLACK SEA

DARDANELLES

E U R O P E

BALTIC SEA

U-BOAT ROUTE

NORTH SEA

Yarmouth
Lowestoft

U-BOAT ROUTE

ATLANTIC OCEAN

Adriatic Sea

U-BOATS

U-BOATS

M E D I T E R R A N E A N   S E A

0   500
Miles

© Arthur Banks 1975

THE DARDANELLES FIASCO IN 1915

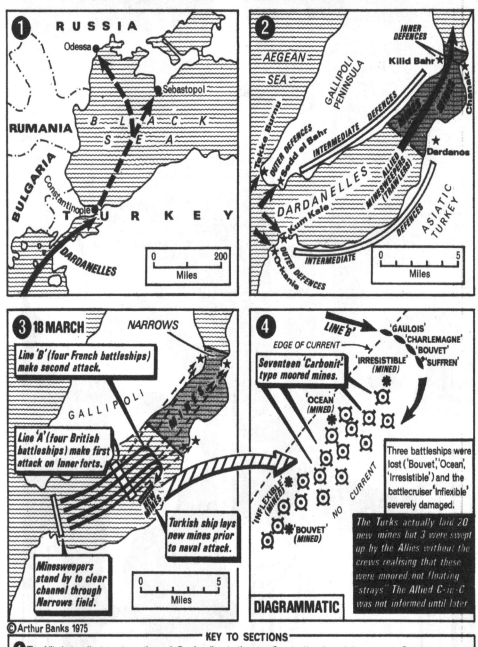

1 R U S S I A

Odessa

Sebastopol

B L A C K S E A

RUMANIA

BULGARIA

Constantinople

T U R K E Y

DARDANELLES

0   200
Miles

2 AEGEAN SEA

INNER DEFENCES

Kilid Bahr

GALLIPOLI PENINSULA

Chanak

OUTER DEFENCES

Tekke Burnu

Sedd el Bahr

INTERMEDIATE DEFENCES

Dardanos

ALLIED MINESWEEPERS (TRAWLERS)

DARDANELLES

Kum Kale

ASIATIC TURKEY

DEFENCES

INTERMEDIATE

Orkanie

OUTER DEFENCES

0   5
Miles

3 18 MARCH   NARROWS

Line 'B' (four French battleships) make second attack.

GALLIPOLI

Line 'A' (four British battleships) make first attack on inner forts.

NEW MINES

Turkish ship lays new mines prior to naval attack.

Minesweepers stand by to clear channel through Narrows field.

0   5
Miles

© Arthur Banks 1975

4 LINE 'B'   GAULOIS

EDGE OF CURRENT   CHARLEMAGNE

'IRRESISTIBLE' (MINED)   'BOUVET'   'SUFFREN'

Seventeen 'Carbonit'-type moored mines.

'OCEAN' (MINED)

NO CURRENT

'INFLEXIBLE' (MINED)

'BOUVET' (MINED)

Three battleships were lost ('Bouvet', 'Ocean', 'Irresistible') and the battlecruiser 'Inflexible' severely damaged.

The Turks actually laid 20 new mines but 3 were swept up by the Allies without the crews realising that these were moored, not floating "strays". The Allied C-in-C was not informed until later.

DIAGRAMMATIC

KEY TO SECTIONS

1 The Allied plan: fleet to steam through Dardanelles to threaten Constantinople and thence on to Russian ports.

2 Stages of plan: (a) destruction of outer defences (b) bombardment of other defences to cover minesweeping phase.

3 Allied fleet enters Dardanelles: bombardment proceeds: disaster overtakes plan when explosions rend warships.

4 Operation abandoned. Diagram illustrates cause of the mystery: group of mines laid at night unknown to Allies.

THE MINESWEEPING PROBLEM AT THE DARDANELLES

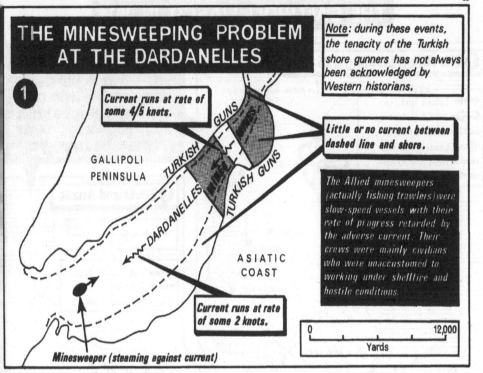

1

Note: during these events, the tenacity of the Turkish shore gunners has not always been acknowledged by Western historians.

Current runs at rate of some 4/5 knots.

GALLIPOLI PENINSULA

TURKISH GUNS

TURKISH GUNS

DARDANELLES

Little or no current between dashed line and shore.

The Allied minesweepers (actually fishing trawlers) were slow-speed vessels with their rate of progress retarded by the adverse current. Their crews were mainly civilians who were unaccustomed to working under shellfire and hostile conditions.

ASIATIC COAST

Current runs at rate of some 2 knots.

Minesweeper (steaming against current)

```
0                           12,000
              Yards
```

2

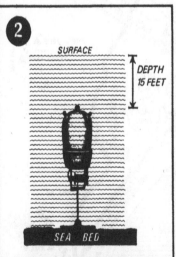

SURFACE

DEPTH 15 FEET

SEA BED

The mines were laid in rows across the Dardanelles, usually at depths of about 15 feet below the surface in calm weather, but these varied in choppy conditions.

3

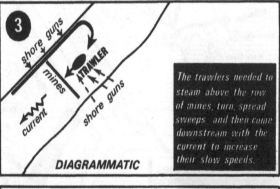

shore guns

mines

TRAWLER

shore guns

current

DIAGRAMMATIC

The trawlers needed to steam above the row of mines, turn, spread sweeps and then come downstream with the current to increase their slow speeds.

4

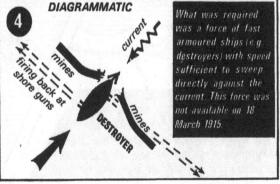

DIAGRAMMATIC

current

mines

firing back at shore guns

mines

DESTROYER

What was required was a force of fast armoured ships (e.g. destroyers) with speed sufficient to sweep directly against the current. This force was not available on 18 March 1915.

THE GALLIPOLI FIASCO IN 1915

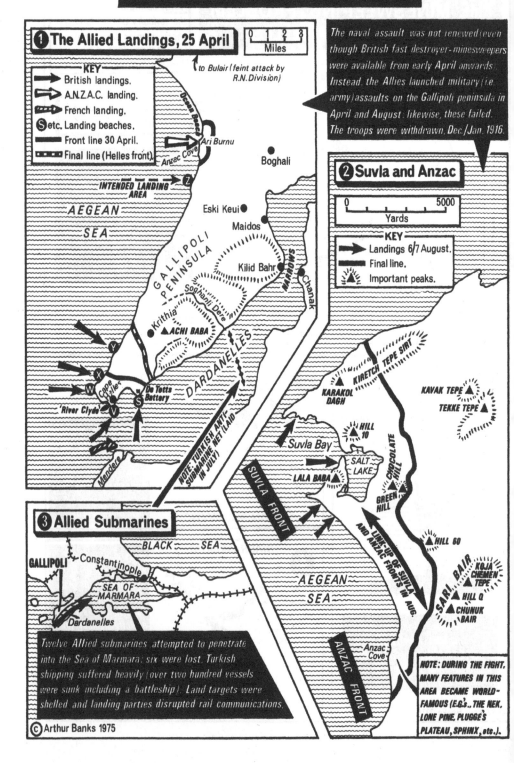

1 The Allied Landings, 25 April

0 1 2 3
Miles

KEY
→ British landings.
⇨ A.N.Z.A.C. landing.
⇛ French landing.
Ⓢ etc. Landing beaches.
▬▬ Front line 30 April.
▭▭▭ Final line (Helles front).

to Bulair (feint attack by
R.N.Division)

The naval assault was not renewed (even though British fast destroyer-minesweepers were available from early April onwards). Instead, the Allies launched military (i.e. army) assaults on the Gallipoli peninsula in April and August; likewise, these failed. The troops were withdrawn, Dec./Jan. 1916.

Ocean Beach
Ari Burnu
Anzac Cove
Boghali

INTENDED LANDING
AREA

AEGEAN
SEA

Eski Keui

Maidos

GALLIPOLI PENINSULA

Kilid Bahr

MARROWS

Chanak

Soghanli Dere

Krithia

▲ACHI BABA

DARDANELLES

Cape Helles

De Totts Battery

'River Clyde'

W

V

S

Menderes

NOTE: TURKISH ANTI-SUBMARINE NET (LAID IN JULY)

2 Suvla and Anzac

0   5000
Yards

KEY
→ Landings 6/7 August.
▬▬ Final line.
▲ Important peaks.

KIRETCH TEPE SIRT

KARAKOL DAGH

KAVAK TEPE ▲

TEKKE TEPE ▲

▲ HILL 10

Suvla Bay

SALT LAKE

CHOCOLATE HILL

LALA BABA

GREEN HILL

SUVLA FRONT

LINK-UP OF SUVLA AND ANZAC FRONTS IN AUG.

▲ HILL 60

SARI BAIR
KOJA CHEMEN TEPE ▲
▲ HILL Q
▲ CHUNUK BAIR

AEGEAN SEA

Anzac Cove

ANZAC FRONT

3 Allied Submarines

BLACK SEA

GALLIPOLI   Constantinople

SEA OF MARMARA

Dardanelles

Twelve Allied submarines attempted to penetrate into the Sea of Marmara: six were lost. Turkish shipping suffered heavily (over two hundred vessels were sunk including a battleship). Land targets were shelled and landing parties disrupted rail communications.

NOTE: DURING THE FIGHT, MANY FEATURES IN THIS AREA BECAME WORLD-FAMOUS (E.G.'s., THE NEK, LONE PINE, PLUGGE'S PLATEAU, SPHINX, etc.).

© Arthur Banks 1975

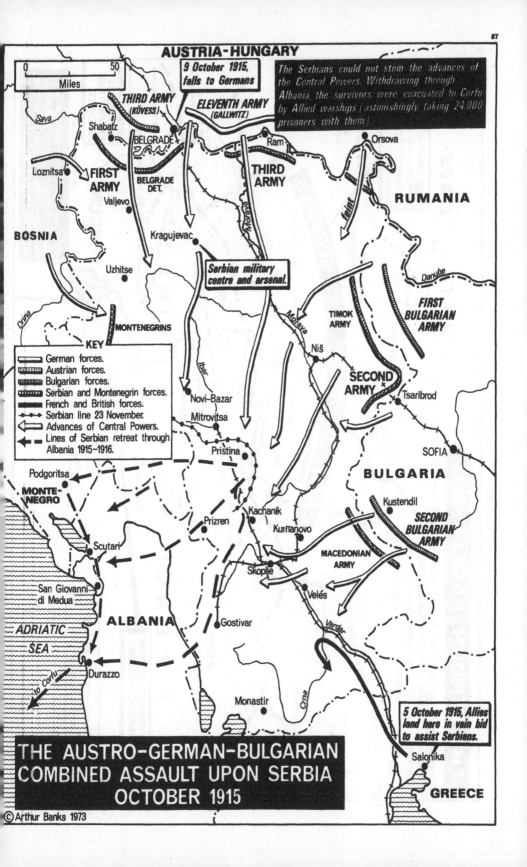

THE AUSTRO-GERMAN-BULGARIAN
COMBINED ASSAULT UPON SERBIA
OCTOBER 1915

© Arthur Banks 1973

THE VERDUN BATTLE 1916

Geographical note: the River Meuse split the front into two sections, thus allowing Germans to launch two consecutive opening attacks.

GERMAN LINES

Note: much of this lost territory was regained by French (October onwards).

FRENCH INNER FORTRESSES STRENGTHEN DEFENCES.

This map shows the extent of the German advance between 21 February and 1 July, when the Allied attack on the Somme front commenced.

AREA OVERRUN BY GERMANS

L I N E S

Maucourt
Damloup
Ft.Tavannes
Ornes
Ft. Douaumont
Ft. Vaux
Ft. Belrupt
Beaumont
Louvemont
Ft. Souville
Ft. St.Michel
Haumont
Bras
Ft. Belleville
Brabant
Ft. Thiaumont
MEUSE
Champneuville
Charny
Champ
Côtes de Meuse
Ft. Vacherauville
Thierville
Consenvoye
Forges
Marre
Ft. Marre
MEUSE
Ft. Cheume
to Bar-le-Duc
Drillancourt
Chattancourt
Ft. Bois Bourrus
Ft. Choisel
Ft. Chana
Montfaucon
Béthincourt
Le Mort Homme
Esnes
Ft. Sartelles
VERDUN

F R E N C H

FRENCH OUTER FORTRESS ZONE GUARDING VERDUN.

Malancourt

Avocourt

KEY
•••• German lines on 21 March.
– – – German lines on 1 July.

Miles
0 1 2 3

© Arthur Banks 1975

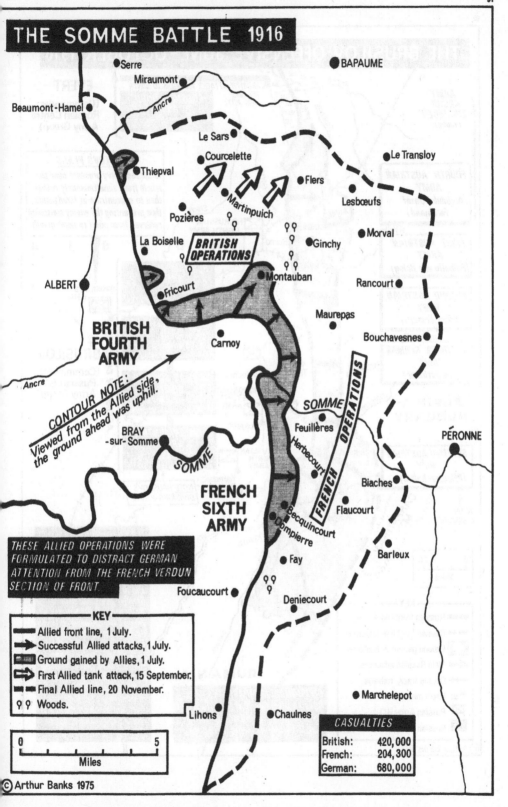

THE SOMME BATTLE 1916

BAPAUME

Serre

Miraumont

Ancre

Beaumont-Hamel

Le Sars

Courcelette

Le Transloy

Thiepval

Flers

Martinpuich

Lesbœufs

Pozières

Morval

La Boiselle

BRITISH OPERATIONS

Ginchy

Montauban

Rancourt

ALBERT

Fricourt

Maurepas

BRITISH FOURTH ARMY

Bouchavesnes

Carnoy

Ancre

CONTOUR NOTE:
Viewed from the Allied side,
the ground ahead was uphill.

SOMME

FRENCH OPERATIONS

Feuillères

BRAY
-sur-Somme

PÉRONNE

SOMME

Herbecourt

FRENCH SIXTH ARMY

Biaches

Flaucourt

Becquincourt
Dompierre

Barleux

THESE ALLIED OPERATIONS WERE
FORMULATED TO DISTRACT GERMAN
ATTENTION FROM THE FRENCH VERDUN
SECTION OF FRONT

Fay

Foucaucourt

Deniecourt

KEY

━━━ Allied front line, 1 July.
➡ Successful Allied attacks, 1 July.
▨ Ground gained by Allies, 1 July.
⇨ First Allied tank attack, 15 September.
▬ ▬ Final Allied line, 20 November.
♀ ♀ Woods.

Marchelepot

Lihons

Chaulnes

CASUALTIES	
British:	420,000
French:	204,300
German:	680,000

0					5

Miles

© Arthur Banks 1975

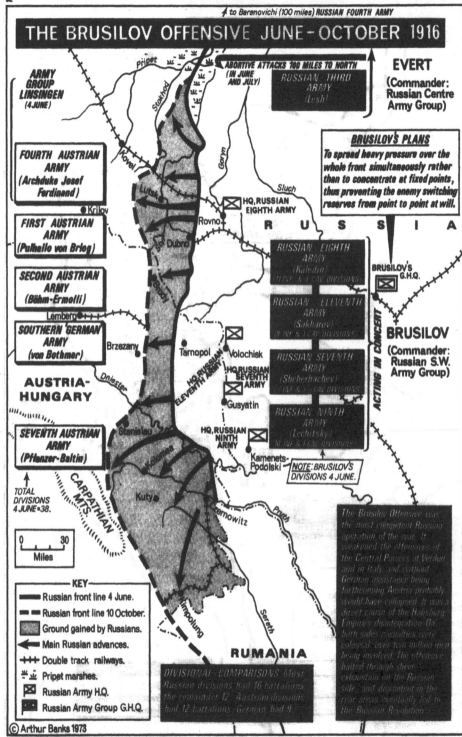

THE BRUSILOV OFFENSIVE JUNE–OCTOBER 1916

to Baranovichi (100 miles) RUSSIAN FOURTH ARMY

EVERT
(Commander: Russian Centre Army Group)

ABORTIVE ATTACKS 100 MILES TO NORTH (IN JUNE AND JULY)

RUSSIAN THIRD ARMY (Lesh)

ARMY GROUP LINSINGEN (4 JUNE)

Pripet

Stokhod

Goryn

Sluch

BRUSILOV'S PLANS
To spread heavy pressure over the whole front simultaneously rather than to concentrate at fixed points, thus preventing the enemy switching reserves from point to point at will.

FOURTH AUSTRIAN ARMY (Archduke Josef Ferdinand)

Kovel

Luga

Krilov

FIRST AUSTRIAN ARMY (Pulhallo von Brlog)

Dubno

Rovno

HQ, RUSSIAN EIGHTH ARMY

R U S S I A

RUSSIAN EIGHTH ARMY (Kaledin) (11 INF. & 3 CAV. DIVISIONS)

BRUSILOV'S G.H.Q.

SECOND AUSTRIAN ARMY (Böhm-Ermolli)

RUSSIAN ELEVENTH ARMY (Sakharov) (8 INF. & 3 CAV. DIVISIONS)

Lemberg

SOUTHERN GERMAN ARMY (von Bothmer)

Brzezany

Tarnopol

Volochisk

HQ RUSSIAN ELEVENTH ARMY

HQ RUSSIAN SEVENTH ARMY

RUSSIAN SEVENTH ARMY (Shcherbachev) (7 INF. & 3 CAV. DIVISIONS)

BRUSILOV
(Commander: Russian S.W. Army Group)

ACTING IN CONCERT

AUSTRIA-HUNGARY

Dniester

Gusyatin

RUSSIAN NINTH ARMY (Lechitsky) (10 INF. & 4 CAV. DIVISIONS)

SEVENTH AUSTRIAN ARMY (Pflanzer-Baltin)

Stanislau

HQ, RUSSIAN NINTH ARMY

Kamenets-Podolski

NOTE: BRUSILOV'S DIVISIONS 4 JUNE.

TOTAL DIVISIONS 4 JUNE = 38.

CARPATHIAN MTS.

Kutya

Czernowitz

Prut

0   30
Miles

Sereth

Kimpolung

KEY
— Russian front line 4 June.
– – Russian front line 10 October.
▓ Ground gained by Russians.
← Main Russian advances.
+++ Double track railways.
⚘ Pripet marshes.
⊠ Russian Army H.Q.
⚑ Russian Army Group G.H.Q.

RUMANIA

DIVISIONAL COMPARISONS: Most Russian divisions had 16 battalions the remainder 12. Austrian divisions had 12 battalions. German had 9.

The Brusilov Offensive was the most competent Russian operation of the war. It weakened the offensives of the Central Powers at Verdun and in Italy and without German assistance being forthcoming Austria probably would have collapsed. It was a direct cause of the Habsburg Empire's disintegration. On both sides casualties were colossal, over two million men being involved. The offensive halted through sheer exhaustion on the Russian side, and discontent in the rear areas eventually led to the Russian Revolution.

© Arthur Banks 1973

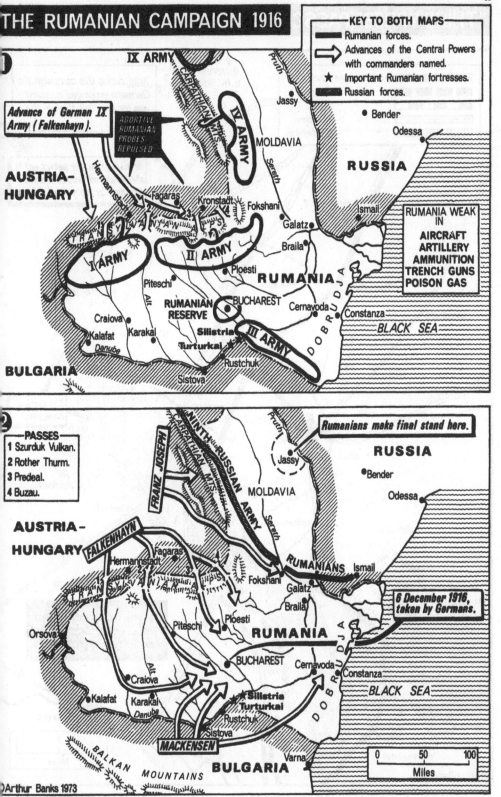

THE RUMANIAN CAMPAIGN 1916

KEY TO BOTH MAPS
- ▬ Rumanian forces.
- ⇨ Advances of the Central Powers with commanders named.
- ★ Important Rumanian fortresses.
- ▨ Russian forces.

①

IX ARMY

Advance of German IX Army (Falkenhayn).

ABORTIVE RUMANIAN PROBES REPULSED

IV ARMY

MOLDAVIA

Jassy

Bender

Odessa

RUSSIA

Ismail

RUMANIA WEAK IN AIRCRAFT ARTILLERY AMMUNITION TRENCH GUNS POISON GAS

AUSTRIA-HUNGARY

Hermannstadt

Fagaras

Kronstadt

Fokshani

Galatz

Braila

TRANSYLVANIA

I ARMY

II ARMY

Piteschi

Ploesti

RUMANIA

DOBRUDJA

RUMANIAN RESERVE

BUCHAREST

Cernavoda

Constanza

BLACK SEA

Craiova

Karakal

Silistria

Turturkai

III ARMY

Kalafat

Danube

Rustchuk

BULGARIA

Sistova

②

PASSES
1 Szurduk Vulkan.
2 Rother Thurm.
3 Predeal.
4 Buzau.

FRANZ JOSEPH

NINTH RUSSIAN ARMY

Rumanians make final stand here.

Jassy

RUSSIA

Bender

Odessa

MOLDAVIA

Sereth

AUSTRIA-HUNGARY

FALKENHAYN

Fagaras

Hermannstadt

TRANSYLVANIA

Fokshani

RUMANIANS

Ismail

Galatz

Braila

6 December 1916, taken by Germans.

Orsova

Piteschi

Ploesti

RUMANIA

DOBRUDJA

Alt

Craiova

BUCHAREST

Cernavoda

Constanza

BLACK SEA

Kalafat

Karakal

Danube

Silistria

Turturkai

Rustchuk

Sistova

MACKENSEN

BALKAN MOUNTAINS

BULGARIA

Varna

0	50	100

Miles

© Arthur Banks 1973

"THIRD YPRES"(PASSCHENDAELE):JULY - NOVEMBER 1917

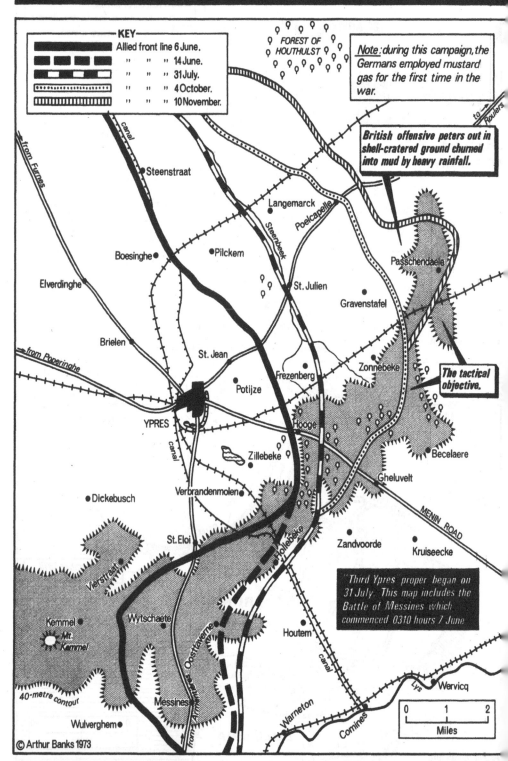

KEY

▬▬▬▬	Allied front line 6 June.
▬ ▬ ▬ ▬	" " " 14 June.
▬□▬□▬□	" " " 31 July.
••••••••	" " " 4 October.
▥▥▥▥▥	" " " 10 November.

FOREST OF HOUTHULST

Note: during this campaign, the Germans employed mustard gas for the first time in the war.

to Roulers

British offensive peters out in shell-cratered ground churned into mud by heavy rainfall.

Steenstraat

Langemarck

Poelcapelle

Boesinghe

Pilckem

Steenbeek

Passchendaele

Elverdinghe

St. Julien

Gravenstafel

Brielen

St. Jean

Frezenberg

Zonnebeke

The tactical objective.

Potijze

YPRES

Hooge

Zillebeke

Becelaere

Gheluvelt

Dickebusch

Verbrandenmolen

MENIN ROAD

St. Eloi

Zandvoorde

Kruiseecke

Kemmel

Wytschaete

Houtem

Mt. Kemmel

Messines

Wervicq

40-metre contour

Lys

Wulverghem

Warneton

Comines

from Furnes

canal

from Poperinghe

canal

Hollebeke

from Armentières

Oostaverne

"Third Ypres proper began on 31 July. This map includes the Battle of Messines which commenced 0310 hours 7 June.

Wytschaete

Vierstraat

0	1	2

Miles

© Arthur Banks 1973

THE BRITISH TANK-SPEARHEADED OFFENSIVE AT CAMBRAI 1917

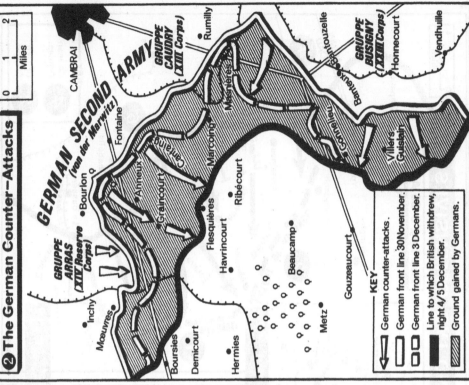

② The German Counter-Attacks

GERMAN SECOND ARMY (von der Marwitz)

GRUPPE CAUDRY (XIII Corps)

GRUPPE BUSSIGNY (XXIII Corps)

GRUPPE ARRAS (XIV Reserve Corps)

CAMBRAI

Rumilly · Sancourt · Honnecourt · Vendhuille · Masnières · Banteux · Gonnelieu · Villers Guislain · Bourlon · Fontaine · Canal · Anneux · Graincourt · Marcoing · Ribécourt · Flesquières · Havrincourt · Beaucamp · Gouzeaucourt · Metz · Inchy · Moeuvres · Boursies · Demicourt · Hermies

KEY
- → German counter-attacks.
- ▭ German front line 30 November.
- ⊏⊐ German front line 3 December.
- ▬ Line to which British withdrew, night 4/5 December.
- ▨ Ground gained by Germans.

0 1 2 Miles

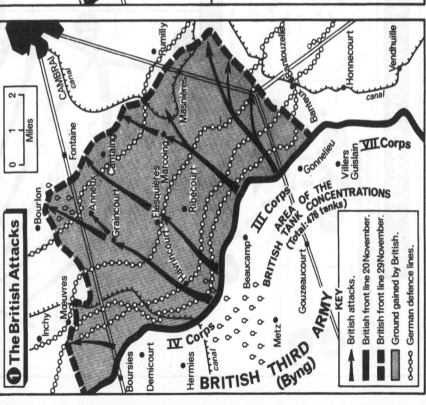

① The British Attacks

CAMBRAI canal

Rumilly · Cantouzelle · Honnecourt · Vendhuille · canal · Masnières · Banteux · Gonnelieu · Villers Guislain · VII Corps · III Corps · AREA OF THE BRITISH TANK CONCENTRATIONS (Total: 476 tanks) · Gouzeaucourt · Fontaine · Bourlon · Anneux · Cantaing · Graincourt · Flesquières · Marcoing · Ribecourt · Havrincourt · Beaucamp · Metz · IV Corps · canal · Inchy · Moeuvres · Boursies · Demicourt · Hermies

BRITISH THIRD ARMY (Byng)

KEY
- → British attacks.
- ▬ British front line 20 November.
- ▐ British front line 29 November.
- ▨ Ground gained by British.
- ∘∘∘ German defence lines.

0 1 2 Miles

© Arthur Banks 1973

THE GERMAN SOMME AND LYS OFFENSIVES 1918

The Lys 9–30 April

Poelcapelle

MENIN ROAD

Hooge

Ypres

Poperinghe

Dickebusch

Messines

Steenwerck

Meteren

Bailleul

Armentières

START LINE

'GEORGETTE'

Fromelles

Aubers

Neuve Chapelle

La Bassée

La Bassée Canal

Cuinchy

Lille Canal

Loos

Estaires

Merville

Béthune

Hinges

MAXIMUM EXTENT OF ADVANCE

German casualties totalled some 348 300

British casualties totalled 260 000

KEY
	German Armies.
4	German Armies.
2	British Armies.

Miles 0 4

Lys

Ypres

Lille

Loos

La Bassée

Lens

Douai

Cambrai

Miraumont

Albert

Péronne

St. Quentin

La Fère

Noyon

Somme

Poperinghe

The Somme 21 March–5 April

Lens

Gavrelle

Douai

Riencourt

Bapaume

Yttres

Miraumont

Combles

Péronne

Albert

Estrees

Chaulnes

Nesle

Ham

Somme

St. Quentin

Noyon

Barisis

Moreuil

Montdidier

Lassigny

'MICHAEL'

START LINE

MAXIMUM EXTENT OF ADVANCE

Arras

Lys

KEY
	German Armies.
6	German Armies.
3	British Armies.

Miles 0 10

© Arthur Banks 1975

THE GERMAN AISNE AND MATZ OFFENSIVES 1918

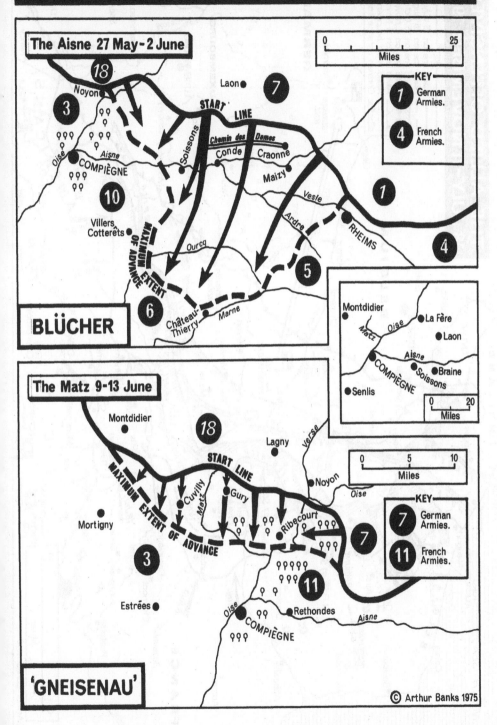

The Aisne 27 May–2 June

18

3

Noyon

Laon ●

7

START LINE

Chemin des Dames

Condé Craonne

Soissons

Oise

Aisne

COMPIÈGNE

Maizy

Vesle

1

10

Villers Cotterêts

RHEIMS

Ardre

4

MAXIMUM EXTENT OF ADVANCE

Ourcq

5

6

Château-Thierry

Marne

BLÜCHER

Miles 0 — 25

KEY

1 German Armies.

4 French Armies.

Montdidier ●

Matz

Oise

● La Fère

● Laon

Aisne

COMPIÈGNE

Soissons ● Braine

● Senlis

Miles 0 — 20

The Matz 9–13 June

Montdidier ●

18

START LINE

Lagny ●

Verse

● Noyon

Oise

MAXIMUM EXTENT OF ADVANCE

Cuvilly

Gury

Matz

Ribecourt

7

● Mortigny

3

11

Estrées ●

Oise

● Rethondes

Aisne

COMPIÈGNE

'GNEISENAU'

Miles 0 — 5 — 10

KEY

7 German Armies.

11 French Armies.

© Arthur Banks 1975

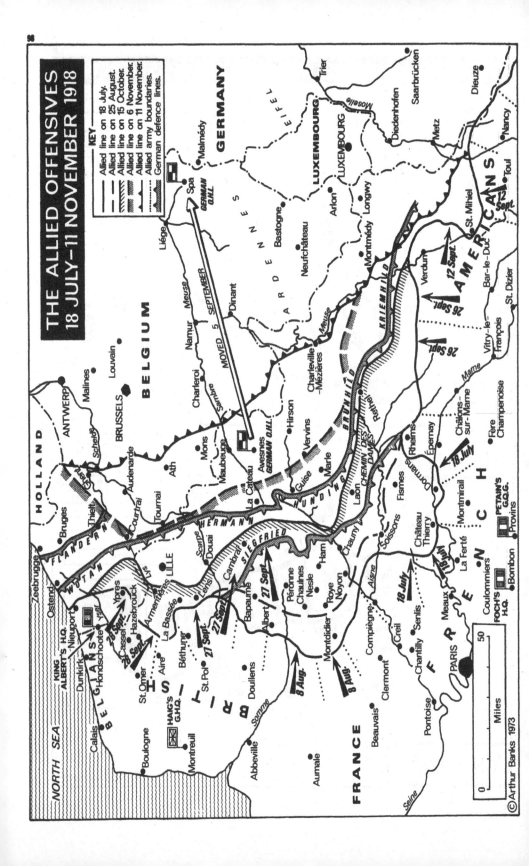

THE ALLIED OFFENSIVES
18 JULY–11 NOVEMBER 1918

KEY

Allied line on 18 July.
Allied line on 25 August.
Allied line on 15 October.
Allied line on 6 November.
Allied line on 11 November.
Allied army boundaries.
German defence lines.

© Arthur Banks 1973

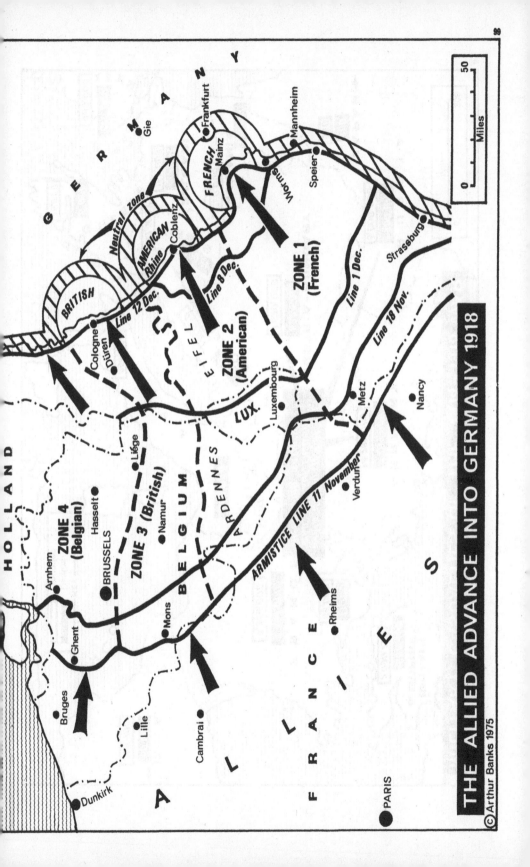

THE ALLIED ADVANCE INTO GERMANY 1918

© Arthur Banks 1975

99

MILITARY CASUALTIES OF THE 1914–1918 WAR

Miles
0 300

KEY
Deaths.
Wounded.

BRITAIN & EMPIRE
908,400
2,090,250

FRANCE
1,358,000
4,350,000

BELG.
13,700
45,000

HOLLAND

GERMANY
1,809,000
4,260,000

MAIN CASUALTIES OF THE WAR ARE SUFFERED BY THESE FOUR NATIONS

AUSTRIA-HUNGARY
922,500
3,630,000

RUSSIA
1,700,000
5,000,000

JAPAN →
300
950

RUMANIA
150,000
335,800

BULGARIA
77,000
153,000

TURKEY
326,000
400,000

GREECE
6,000
25,000

SERBIA
48,000
133,500

ALBANIA

MONTENEGRO
3,000
10,000

ITALY
463,000
954,000

SWITZ.

U.S.A.
50,600
205,700

© Arthur Banks 1975

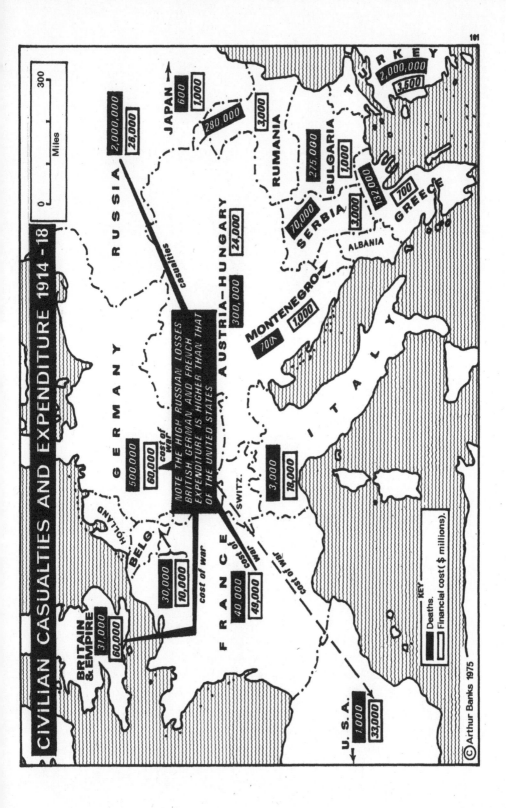

CIVILIAN CASUALTIES AND EXPENDITURE 1914 - 18

KEY:
▮ Deaths.
▯ Financial cost ($ millions).

NOTE THE HIGH RUSSIAN LOSSES. BRITISH GERMAN AND FRENCH EXPENDITURE IS HIGHER THAN THAT OF THE UNITED STATES

Miles
0   300

RUSSIA
2,000,000
26,000

JAPAN →
600
1,000

280,000
3,000

TURKEY
2,000,000
3,500

RUMANIA
275 000
1,000

BULGARIA
132 000

GREECE
700

SERBIA
70,000
3,000

AUSTRIA–HUNGARY
24,000
300,000

MONTENEGRO
700
1,000

ALBANIA

GERMANY
500,000
60,000
cost of war

casualties

SWITZ.
3,000
18,000

ITALY

HOLLAND
BELG.
30,000
10,000
cost of war

FRANCE
40,000
49,000
cost of war

cost of war

BRITAIN & EMPIRE
31,000
60,000

U.S.A.
1,000
33,000

101

© Arthur Banks 1975

V
THE INTER-WAR YEARS

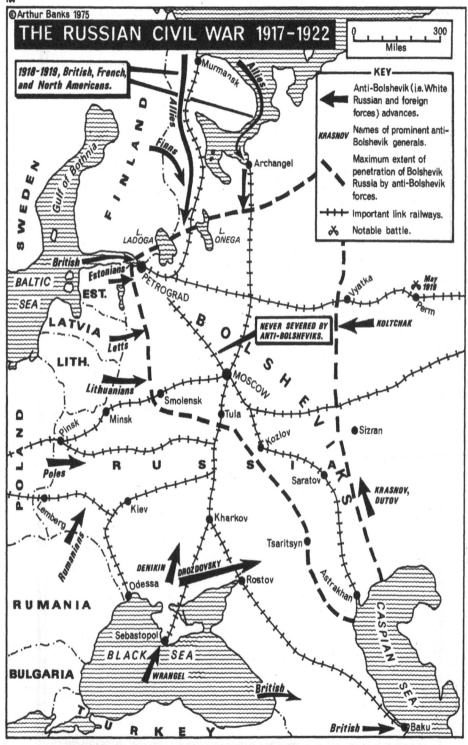

THE RUSSIAN CIVIL WAR 1917-1922

0   300
Miles

1918-1919, British, French, and North Americans.

SWEDEN

Gulf of Bothnia

FINLAND

Murmansk

Allies

Allies

Archangel

Finns

L. LADOGA

L. ONEGA

British

BALTIC SEA

Estonians

EST.

PETROGRAD

LATVIA

Letts

LITH.

Lithuanians

POLAND

Poles

Pinsk

Minsk

Smolensk

MOSCOW

Tula

Lemberg

Kiev

Kharkov

Rumanians

RUMANIA

Odessa

DENIKIN

DROZDOVSKY

Rostov

Sebastopol

BLACK SEA

WRANGEL

BULGARIA

TURKEY

British

British

Baku

Vyatka

May 1919

Perm

NEVER SEVERED BY ANTI-BOLSHEVIKS.

KOLTCHAK

BOLSHEVIKS

Sizran

Kozlov

Saratov

KRASNOV, DUTOV

Tsaritsyn

Astrakhan

CASPIAN SEA

RUSSIA

KEY

Anti-Bolshevik (i.e. White Russian and foreign forces) advances.

KRASNOV   Names of prominent anti-Bolshevik generals.

Maximum extent of penetration of Bolshevik Russia by anti-Bolshevik forces.

╬╬╬   Important link railways.

✂   Notable battle.

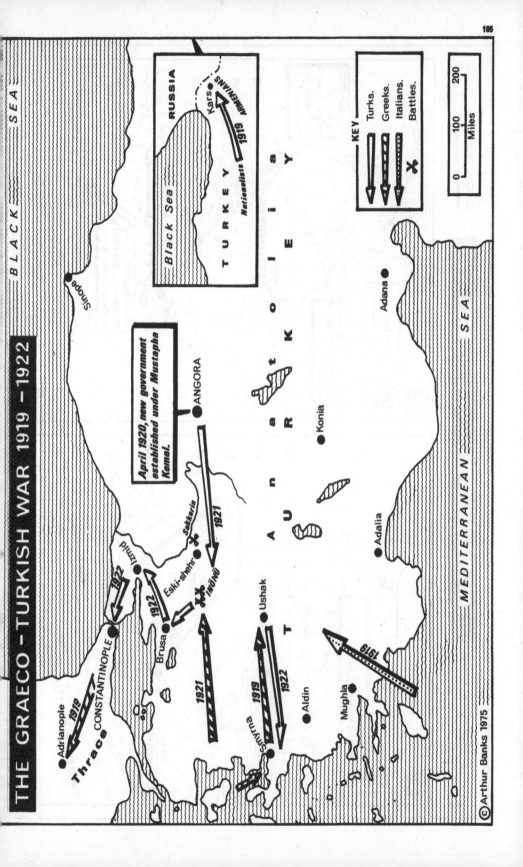

THE GRAECO–TURKISH WAR 1919–1922

BLACK SEA

Sinope

Thrace

Adrianople

CONSTANTINOPLE

1919

1922

Izmid

1922

Brusa

Eski-shehr

Sakkaria

İNÖNÜ

1921

ANGORA

April 1920, new government established under Mustapha Kemal.

RUSSIA

Kars

1919 ARMENIANS

TURKEY

Nationalists

Black Sea

A n a t o l i a

T U R K E Y

Konia

Adana

Adalia

Ushak

Aldin

Mughla

Smyrna

1919

1922

1921

1919

MEDITERRANEAN

SEA

KEY

Turks.
Greeks.
Italians.
Battles.

0   100   200
Miles

© Arthur Banks 1975

THE RUSSO–POLISH WAR 1920

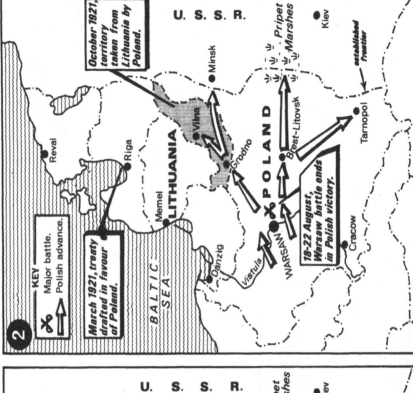

KEY
- ✗ Major battle.
- ⬆ Polish advance.

⬆ Poles.
⬇ Russians.

October 1921, territory taken from Lithuania by Poland.

March 1921, treaty drafted in favour of Poland.

18–22 August, Warsaw battle ends in Polish victory.

established frontier

U. S. S. R.

Kiev

Pripet Marshes

Minsk

Brest-Litovsk

Tarnopol

POLAND

Vila

Grodno

WARSAW

Vistula

Danzig

Memel

LITHUANIA

Riga

Reval

BALTIC SEA

Cracow

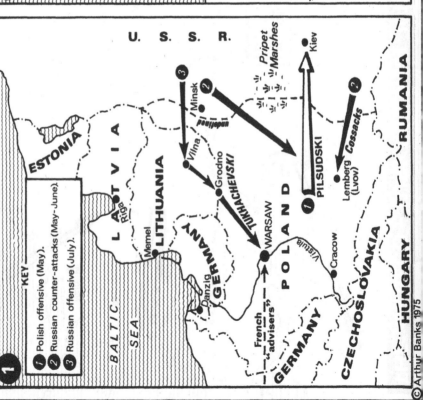

KEY
- ① Polish offensive (May).
- ② Russian counter-attacks (May–June).
- ③ Russian offensive (July).

0 ——— 100
Miles

U. S. S. R.

Pripet Marshes

Kiev

Minsk

Vilna

Grodno

TUKHACHEVSKI

WARSAW

PILSUDSKI

Lemberg (Lvov)

Cossacks

Vistula

Cracow

POLAND

GERMANY

Danzig

Memel

LITHUANIA

L A T V I A

Riga

ESTONIA

BALTIC SEA

French "advisers"

CZECHOSLOVAKIA

HUNGARY

RUMANIA

GERMANY

© Arthur Banks 1975

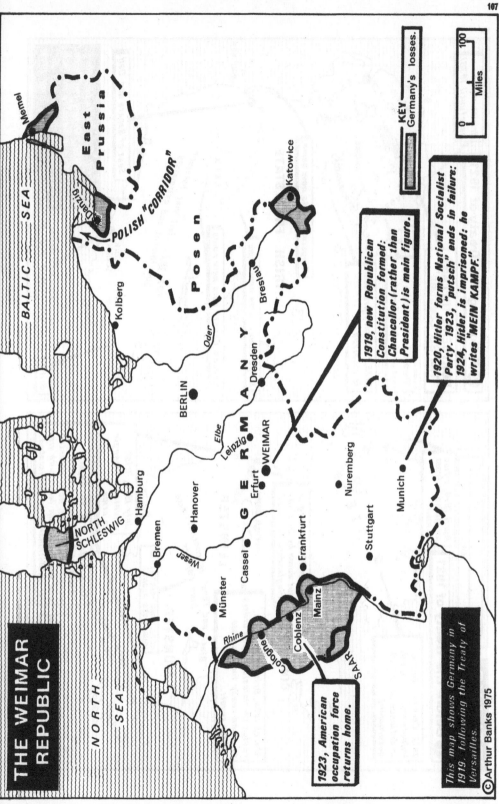

THE WEIMAR REPUBLIC

KEY
Germany's losses.

0   100
Miles

1919, new Republican Constitution formed: Chancellor (rather than President) is main figure.

1920, Hitler forms National Socialist Party. 1923, "putsch" ends in failure: 1924, Hitler is imprisoned: he writes "MEIN KAMPF."

1923, American occupation force returns home.

BALTIC SEA

Memel

East Prussia

Danzig

POLISH "CORRIDOR"

Kolberg

Posen

Oder

Katowice

Breslau

Dresden

BERLIN

Elbe

Leipzig

WEIMAR

Erfurt

Nuremberg

Munich

G E R M A N Y

NORTH SCHLESWIG

Hamburg

Bremen

Weser

Hanover

Münster

Cassel

Frankfurt

Stuttgart

Mainz

Coblenz

Cologne

Rhine

SAAR

NORTH SEA

This map shows Germany in 1919 following the Treaty of Versailles.

© Arthur Banks 1975

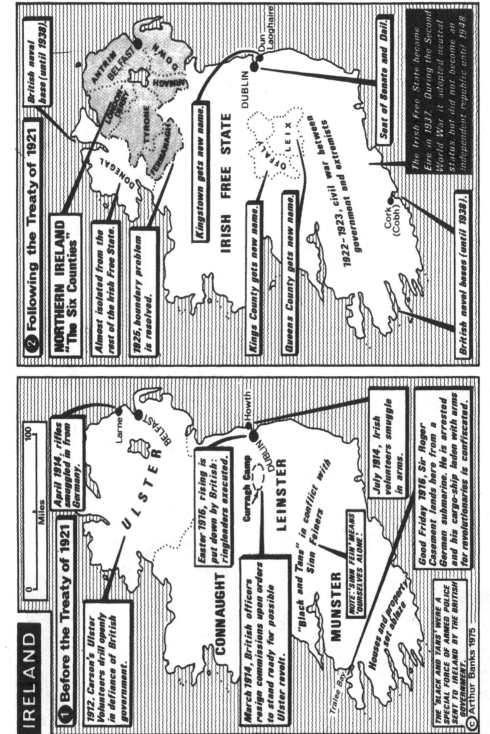

ITALIAN EXPANSION 1889-1939

1939, annexed to Italy.

1919, ceded to Italy by Austria.

1919-1924, disputed with Yugoslavia.

1919-1921, occupied by volunteer patriots; 1924, Italian.

1912, occupied by Italy.

Black Sea

ALBANIA

Sardinia

Sicily

Mediterranean Sea

Dodecanese Islands

Abortive attempt to establish control of Smyrna-Adalia region in 1919.

L I B Y A

1912-1925, ceded to Italy by Britain.

1911-1912, conquered by Italy from Ottoman Empire.

Red Sea

1890, declared an Italian province.

Italian from 1889.

1919, ceded to Italy by France.

1912, conquered by Italy (but not completely pacified until 1931).

ERITREA

1935-1936, conquered by Italy.

A B Y S S I N I A

ITALIAN SOMALILAND

1925, ceded to Italy by Britain.

0   500
Miles

© Arthur Banks 1975

INDIAN OCEAN

EUROPE IN 1925

Note the extent of Germany; also, Austria-Hungary no longer exists as such. Russia is now U.S.S.R.

© Arthur Banks 1975

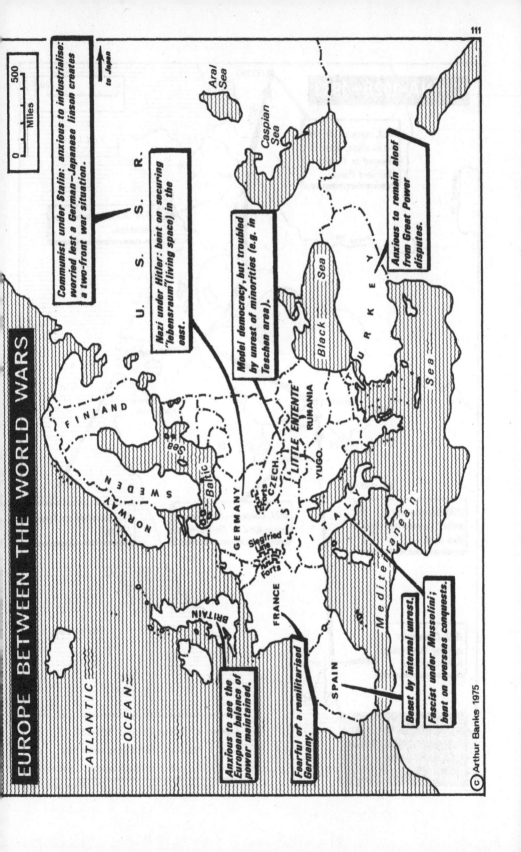

EUROPE BETWEEN THE WORLD WARS

Communist under Stalin: anxious to industrialise;
worried lest a German–Japanese liason creates
a two-front war situation.

Nazi under Hitler: bent on securing
"lebensraum"(living space) in the
east.

Model democracy, but troubled
by unrest of minorities (e.g. in
Teschen area).

Anxious to remain aloof
from Great Power
disputes.

Anxious to see the
European balance of
power maintained.

Fearful of a remilitarised
Germany.

Beset by internal unrest.

Fascist under Mussolini;
bent on overseas conquests.

ATLANTIC

OCEAN

FINLAND

NORWAY

SWEDEN

Baltic Sea

GERMANY

Siegfried
Line
Forts

BRITAIN

FRANCE

SPAIN

Mediterranean Sea

ITALY

CZECH.

Forts

"LITTLE ENTENTE"

YUGO.

RUMANIA

Black Sea

TURKEY

Caspian Sea

Aral Sea

U. S. S. R.

to Japan

0   500
Miles

© Arthur Banks 1975

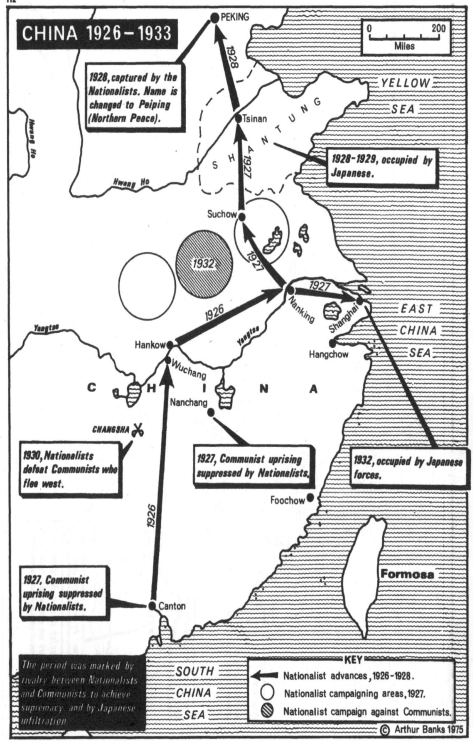

112

CHINA 1926-1933

0 ___ 200
Miles

PEKING

1928, captured by the Nationalists. Name is changed to Peiping (Northern Peace).

1928

Hwang Ho

Hwang Ho

S H A N T U N G

YELLOW SEA

Tsinan

1928-1929, occupied by Japanese.

1927

Suchow

1932

1927

Nanking

1927

Shanghai

EAST CHINA SEA

1926

Yangtse

Hankow

Yangtse

Wuchang

Hangchow

C   H   I   N   A

Nanchang

CHANGSHA ✂

1930, Nationalists defeat Communists who flee west.

1927, Communist uprising suppressed by Nationalists.

1932, occupied by Japanese forces.

1926

Foochow

Formosa

1927, Communist uprising suppressed by Nationalists.

Canton

The period was marked by rivalry between Nationalists and Communists to achieve supremacy, and by Japanese infiltration.

SOUTH CHINA SEA

KEY

⟵ Nationalist advances, 1926-1928.

◯ Nationalist campaigning areas, 1927.

▨ Nationalist campaign against Communists.

© Arthur Banks 1975

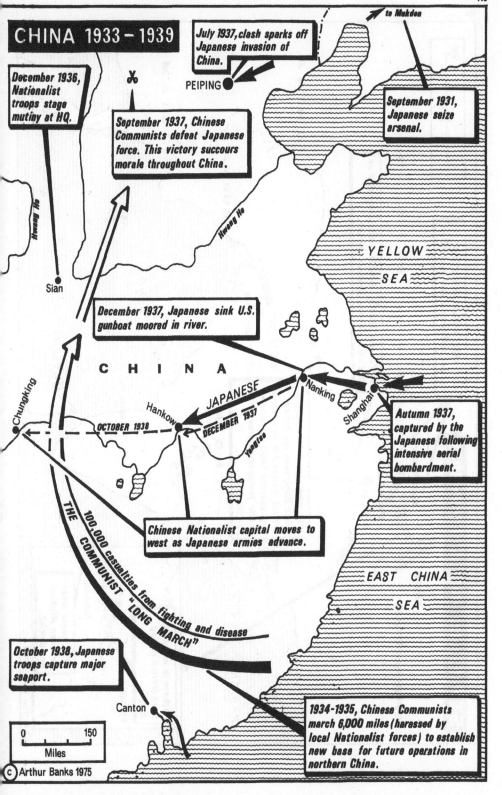

CHINA 1933 – 1939

July 1937, clash sparks off Japanese invasion of China.

to Mukden

PEIPING

December 1936, Nationalist troops stage mutiny at HQ.

September 1937, Chinese Communists defeat Japanese force. This victory succours morale throughout China.

September 1931, Japanese seize arsenal.

Hwang Ho

Hwang Ho

YELLOW SEA

Sian

December 1937, Japanese sink U.S. gunboat moored in river.

C H I N A

JAPANESE

Nanking

Shanghai

Chungking

OCTOBER 1938

Hankow

DECEMBER 1937

Yangtse

Autumn 1937, captured by the Japanese following intensive aerial bombardment.

Chinese Nationalist capital moves to west as Japanese armies advance.

100,000 casualties from fighting and disease

THE COMMUNIST "LONG MARCH"

EAST CHINA SEA

October 1938, Japanese troops capture major seaport.

Canton

1934-1935, Chinese Communists march 6,000 miles (harassed by local Nationalist forces) to establish new base for future operations in northern China.

0   150
Miles

© Arthur Banks 1975

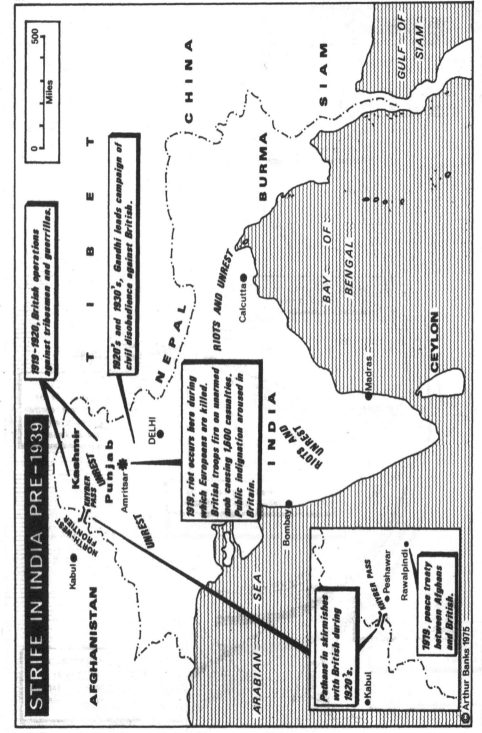

STRIFE IN INDIA PRE-1939

1919-1920, British operations against tribesmen and guerrillas.

1920's and 1930's, Gandhi leads campaign of civil disobedience against British.

1919, riot occurs here during which Europeans are killed. British troops fire on unarmed mob causing 1,600 casualties. Public indignation aroused in Britain.

Pathans in skirmishes with British during 1920's.

1919, peace treaty between Afghans and British.

RIOTS AND UNREST

RIOTS AND UNREST

UNREST

UNREST

AFGHANISTAN
Kabul●

NORTH-WEST FRONTIER

KHYBER PASS

Kashmir

Punjab
Amritsar✳

DELHI●

NEPAL

TIBET

CHINA

BURMA

SIAM

GULF OF SIAM

BAY OF BENGAL

Calcutta●

Madras●

Bombay●

ARABIAN SEA

CEYLON

●Kabul
KHYBER PASS
●Peshawar
Rawalpindi●

500
0
Miles

© Arthur Banks 1975

SPAIN: THE AXIS "TRAINING GROUND" 1936–1939

The Spanish Civil War between the Nationalists and Republicans attracted foreign contingents and volunteers to both sides. The Nationalists were the victors. Total casualties at least 750 000.

KEY

R Military revolts, 1936.
→ Spanish Nationalist advances.
---→ Spanish government moves from Madrid to east coast.
⇨ Spanish Nationalist naval blockade (from Nov. 1937).
✳ Important battles.
❋ Heavily bombed by Germans.

September 1937, nine-power conference held at Nyon in Switzerland: anti-submarine naval patrol zones established.

Mid-1937, submarines of "unknown" origin attack British, French, Soviet, and Spanish Government shipping.

MEDITERRANEAN SEA

Balearic Islands

Non-interventionist policy.

26 January 1939, falls to Nationalists.

Barcelona

Oct. 1937

1939

Ebro

Vinaroz

1939

Valencia

1938

Teruel

December 1937–February 1938. bitter fighting here.

March 1937, Italian reverses.

Brihuega
Guadalajara

Nov. 1936

1937–1938

28 March 1939, both cities surrender to Nationalists: civil war ends.

May 1937, shelled by German pocket-battleship: bombed by German Air Force.

July 1936, Franco arrives here to command Spanish Nationalist forces.

April 1937, devastated by German aircraft.

Guernica ❋

Bilbao ●

1937

OVIEDO R

BURGOS R

1938

MADRID ❋ R

TOLEDO

Besieged at intervals, 1936–1939.

Nationalist HQ.

Duero

Almeria ❋

Malaga

SEVILLE R

Guadalquivir

SPAIN

Badajoz ●

1936

1936

Tagus

1936

SPANISH MOROCCO

CADIZ R

1936

Melilla ●

P O R T U G A L

LISBON ●

1928, dictatorship established.

F R A N C E

Andorra

0   100
Miles

© Arthur Banks 1975

VI
THE SECOND
WORLD WAR

HITLER'S ROAD TO WAR 1936-1939

KEY

- ⌘ Hitler's "Third Reich".
- --→ Training ground for Luftwaffe (in Spain).
- ① Hitler's first "exploratory" move (1936).
- ② Austria annexed (1938).
- ③ Sudetenland annexed (later, western Czechoslovakia, 1939).
- ④ Memel annexed (1939).
- ▨ Territories gained by Hitler (1936-1939).
- ⑤ Danzig attacked (September 1939).

U. S. S. R.

LATVIA
LITHUANIA
Memel
EAST PRUSSIA (GERMANY)
Danzig
POLAND
CZECHO-SLOVAKIA
HUNGARY
RUMANIA
BULGARIA
ALB.
YUGOSLAVIA
AUSTRIA
SWITZ.
ITALY
ROME
SWEDEN
BALTIC SEA
Berlin
Sudetenland
Rhineland
Rhine
DENMARK
BELGIUM
LUX.
FRANCE
BRITAIN
SPAIN
Miles
0   500

MUSSOLINI
Hitler's ally and friend

© Arthur Banks 1975

THE INVASION OF POLAND BY GERMANY (1 SEPTEMBER) & U.S.S.R. (17 SEPTEMBER) 1939

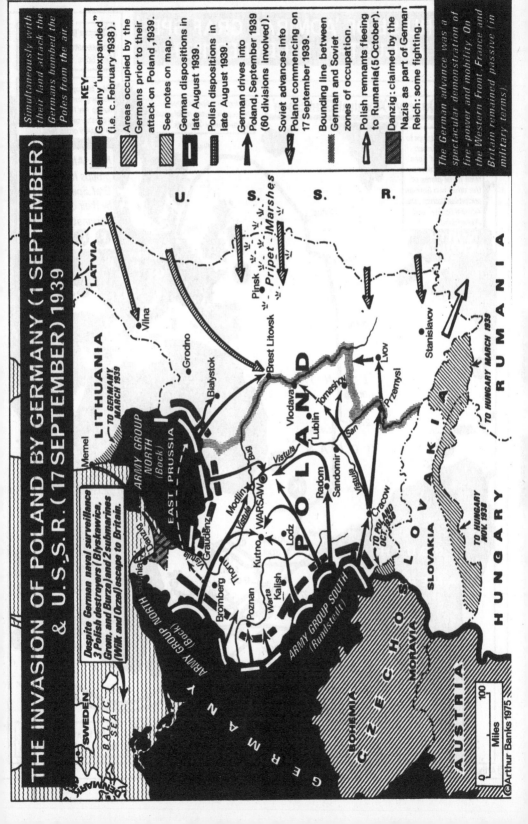

Simultaneously with their land attack the Germans bombed the Poles from the air.

KEY

- Germany "unexpanded" (i.e. c.February 1938).
- Areas occupied by the Germans prior to their attack on Poland, 1939.
- See notes on map.
- German dispositions in late August 1939.
- Polish dispositions in late August 1939.
- German drives into Poland, September 1939 (60 divisions involved).
- Soviet advances into Poland commencing on 17 September 1939.
- Bounding line between German and Soviet zones of occupation.
- Polish remnants fleeing to Rumania(5 October).
- Danzig: claimed by the Nazis as part of German Reich: some fighting.

The German advance was a spectacular demonstration of fire-power and mobility On the Western Front France and Britain remained passive (in military terms).

Despite German naval surveillance 3 Polish destroyers (Blyskawica, Grom, and Burza) and 2 submarines (Wilk and Orzel) escape to Britain.

©Arthur Banks 1975.

THE CRUISE OF 'ADMIRAL GRAF SPEE' 21 AUGUST-13 DECEMBER 1939

KEY
Track of German pocket-battleship 'Admiral Graf Spee', with dates.

Total tonnage of merchant shipping sunk by 'Graf Spee' during her 115-day cruise as a commerce raider amounted to 50,089 gross tons.

❶ The Quarry-'Admiral Graf Spee'

During 'Graf Spee's' voyage, her supplies were replenished by the tanker 'Altmark'.

Note: Allied naval groups hunting the 'Graf Spee' are shown by their official force designations, thus.... ⓕ ⓖ ⓗ etc.

Note: in an attempt to confuse the British Admiralty, 'Graf Spee' frequently displayed false name-plates of the other two German pocket-battleships, the 'Admiral Scheer' and 'Deutschland'.

NORTH AMERICA

GERMANY
Wilhelmshaven

EUROPE

23 Aug.
25 Aug.
21 Aug.
27 Aug.
29 Aug.
31 Aug.
2 Sept.
4 Sept.
6 Sept.
8 Sept.

ⓛ

ⓙ

A T L A N T I C

O C E A N

AFRICA

ⓕ

ⓝ

ⓜ

ⓚ

SOUTH AMERICA

INDIAN OCEAN

30 Sept.
29 Sept.
10 Sept.
10 Oct.
8 Oct.
3 Oct.
5 Oct.
7 Oct.
13 Oct.
23 Oct.
22 Oct.
2 Dec.
27 Sept.
17 Sept.
2 Dec.
3 Dec.
7 Dec.
4 Dec.
16 Nov.
14 Nov.
ⓖ
13 Dec.
28 Oct.
7 Dec.
24 Nov.
ⓗ
1 Nov.
20 Nov.
8 Nov.
ⓘ

Plate

13 December 1939, the Battle of the River Plate.

VICTIMS OF THE 'GRAF SPEE'

❶ SS 'Clement' ❷ SS 'Newton Beech' ❸ SS 'Ashlea' ❹ SS 'Huntsman'
❺ SS 'Trevanion' ❻ SS 'Africa Shell' ❼ SS 'Doric Star' ❽ SS 'Tairoa' ❾ SS 'Streonshalh'

© Arthur Banks 1975

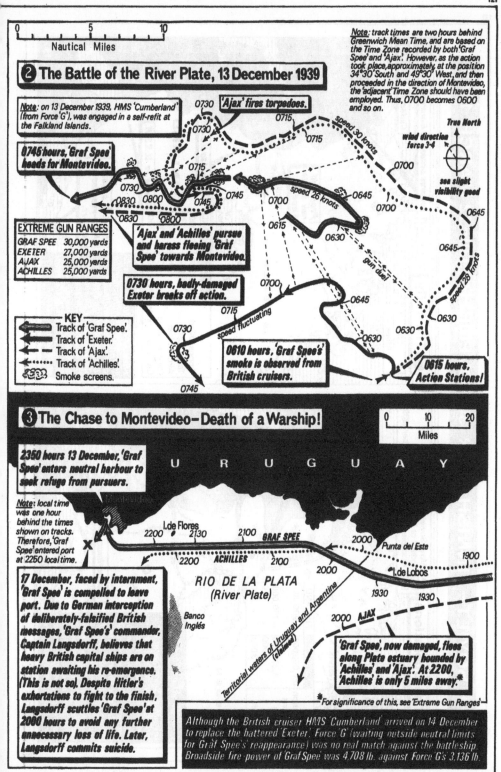

Note: track times are two hours behind Greenwich Mean Time, and are based on the Time Zone recorded by both 'Graf Spee' and 'Ajax'. However, as the action took place, approximately, at the position 34°30'South and 49°30'West, and then proceeded in the direction of Montevideo, the 'adjacent' Time Zone should have been employed. Thus, 0700 becomes 0600 and so on.

❷ The Battle of the River Plate, 13 December 1939

Note: on 13 December 1939, HMS 'Cumberland' (from Force 'G'), was engaged in a self-refit at the Falkland Islands.

'Ajax' fires torpedoes.

0745 hours, 'Graf Spee' heads for Montevideo.

speed 30 knots

True North

wind direction force 3-4

sea slight visibility good

speed 26 knots

speed 28 knots

gun duel

EXTREME GUN RANGES
GRAF SPEE	30,000 yards
EXETER	27,000 yards
AJAX	25,000 yards
ACHILLES	25,000 yards

'Ajax' and 'Achilles' pursue and harass fleeing 'Graf Spee' towards Montevideo.

0730 hours, badly-damaged Exeter breaks off action.

speed fluctuating

KEY
Track of 'Graf Spee'.
Track of 'Exeter.'
Track of 'Ajax'.
Track of 'Achilles'.
Smoke screens.

0610 hours, 'Graf Spee's' smoke is observed from British cruisers.

0615 hours, Action Stations!

❸ The Chase to Montevideo – Death of a Warship!

2350 hours 13 December, 'Graf Spee' enters neutral harbour to seek refuge from pursuers.

Note: local time was one hour behind the times shown on tracks. Therefore, 'Graf Spee' entered port at 2250 local time.

17 December, faced by internment, 'Graf Spee' is compelled to leave port. Due to German interception of deliberately-falsified British messages, 'Graf Spee's' commander, Captain Langsdorff, believes that heavy British capital ships are on station awaiting his re-emergence. (This is not so). Despite Hitler's exhortations to fight to the finish, Langsdorff scuttles 'Graf Spee' at 2000 hours to avoid any further unnecessary loss of life. Later, Langsdorff commits suicide.

U R U G U A Y

Miles

I. de Flores
2200   2130   2100   **GRAF SPEE**   2000   Punta del Este   1900

2200   **ACHILLES**   2100   2000   I. de Lobos

RIO DE LA PLATA
(River Plate)

Banco Inglés

1930   1930

2000   **AJAX**

Territorial waters of Uruguay and Argentina (claimed)

'Graf Spee', now damaged, flees along Plate estuary hounded by 'Achilles' and 'Ajax'. At 2200, 'Achilles' is only 5 miles away.*

*For significance of this, see 'Extreme Gun Ranges'

Although the British cruiser HMS 'Cumberland' arrived on 14 December to replace the battered 'Exeter', Force 'G' (waiting outside neutral limits for Graf Spee's reappearance) was no real match against the battleship. Broadside fire-power of 'Graf Spee' was 4,708 lb. against Force G's 3,136 lb.

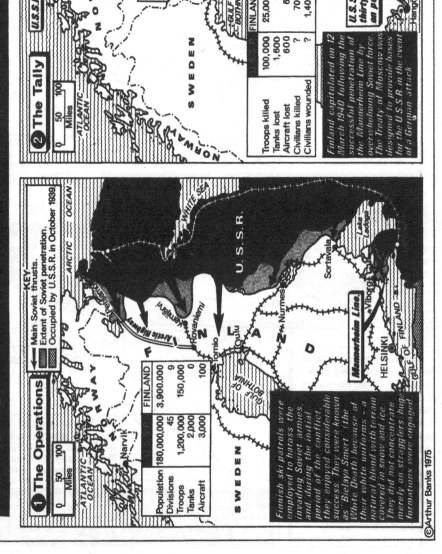

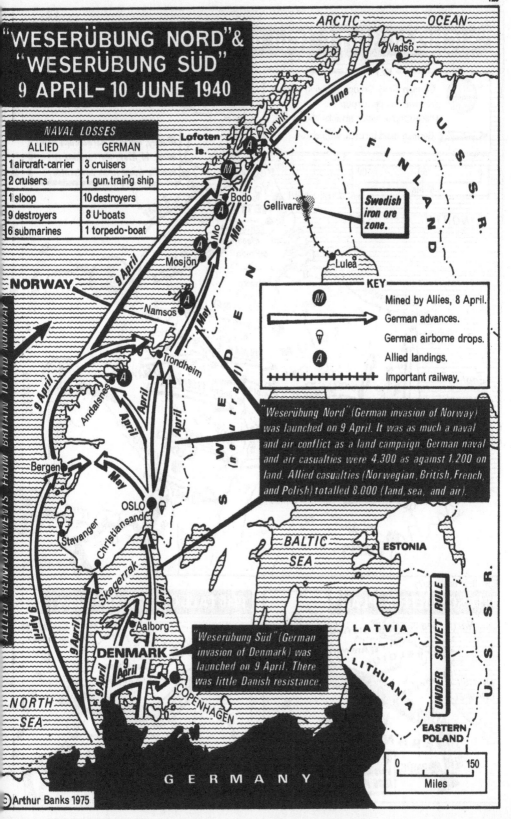

"WESERÜBUNG NORD" & "WESERÜBUNG SÜD" 9 APRIL – 10 JUNE 1940

ARCTIC OCEAN

Vadsö

NAVAL LOSSES

ALLIED	GERMAN
1 aircraft-carrier	3 cruisers
2 cruisers	1 gun.train'g ship
1 sloop	10 destroyers
9 destroyers	8 U-boats
6 submarines	1 torpedo-boat

June

Narvik

Lofoten Is.

FINLAND

U.S.S.R.

Bodö

Gellivare

Swedish iron ore zone.

Mo

Mosjön

S W E D E N (neutral)

Luleå

Namsos

KEY

M — Mined by Allies, 8 April.

→ — German advances.

⚑ — German airborne drops.

A — Allied landings.

++++ — Important railway.

Trondheim

Andalsnes

April

"Weserübung Nord" (German invasion of Norway) was launched on 9 April. It was as much a naval and air conflict as a land campaign. German naval and air casualties were 4,300 as against 1,200 on land. Allied casualties (Norwegian, British, French, and Polish) totalled 8,000 (land, sea, and air).

Bergen

May

OSLO

Stavanger

Christiansand

Skagerrak

BALTIC SEA

ESTONIA

LATVIA

LITHUANIA

U.S.S.R.

UNDER SOVIET RULE

Aalborg

9 April

DENMARK

9 April

"Weserübung Süd" (German invasion of Denmark) was launched on 9 April. There was little Danish resistance.

COPENHAGEN

NORTH SEA

EASTERN POLAND

ALLIED REINFORCEMENTS FROM BRITAIN TO AID NORWAY

NORWAY

9 April

GERMANY

© Arthur Banks 1975

0	150

Miles

124

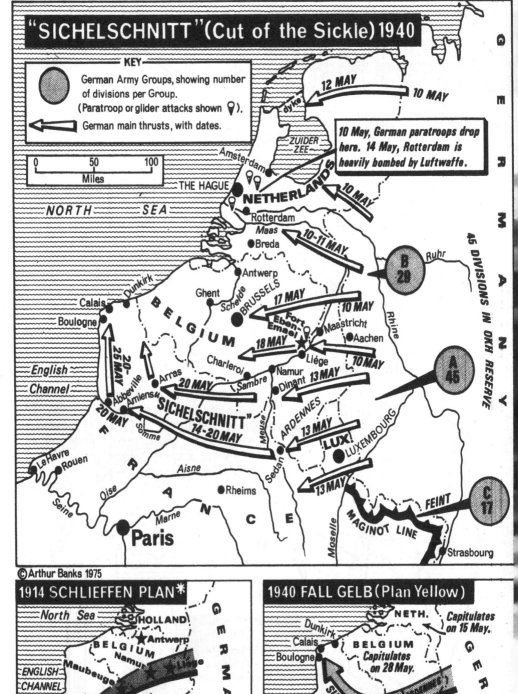

"SICHELSCHNITT" (Cut of the Sickle) 1940

KEY

German Army Groups, showing number of divisions per Group.
(Paratroop or glider attacks shown ♥).

German main thrusts, with dates.

0   50   100
Miles

10 May, German paratroops drop here. 14 May, Rotterdam is heavily bombed by Luftwaffe.

G E R M A N Y

45 DIVISIONS IN OKH RESERVE

12 MAY
10 MAY
dyke
ZUIDER ZEE
Amsterdam
THE HAGUE
NETHERLANDS
10 MAY
NORTH   SEA
Rotterdam
Maas
Breda
10-11 MAY
B 20
Ruhr
Antwerp
Dunkirk
Ghent   Schelde   BRUSSELS
17 MAY
10 MAY
Calais
BELGIUM
Fort Eben-Emael
Maastricht
Rhine
Boulogne
18 MAY
Aachen
English
Charleroi   Liége
10 MAY
Channel
Arras   Namur
Abbeville   Sambre   Dinant
13 MAY
A 45
20 MAY
20-25 MAY
Amiens
20 MAY
"SICHELSCHNITT"
ARDENNES
13 MAY
F
Somme
14-20 MAY
Meuse
LUX.
LUXEMBOURG
Le Havre
Rouen
R
Aisne
Sedan
13 MAY
Seine   Oise   A
Rheims
N   C   E
FEINT
C 17
Marne
MAGINOT LINE
Paris
Moselle
Strasbourg

© Arthur Banks 1975

1914 SCHLIEFFEN PLAN ✱

North Sea
HOLLAND
Antwerp
BELGIUM
Namur   Liége
Maubeuge
ENGLISH CHANNEL
G E R M A N Y
F R A N C E
LUX.
UNSUCCESSFUL
PARIS

✱ Moltke's 1914 version of original 1905 Plan.

1940 FALL GELB (Plan Yellow)

NETH.
Capitulates on 15 May.
Dunkirk
Calais
BELGIUM
Boulogne
Capitulates on 28 May.
G E R M A N Y
SUCCESSFUL
later
PARIS
Maginot Line
F R A N C E

Inspired by Manstein.

OPERATIONS IN THE VICINITY OF DUNKIRK IN 1940

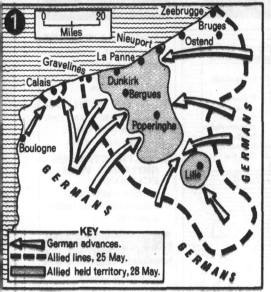

1

0   20
Miles

Zeebrugge
Bruges
Nieuport   Ostend
Gravelines
Calais   Dunkirk
Bergues
Boulogne   Poperinghe
Lille

GERMANS

GERMANS

GERMANS

KEY
German advances.
Allied lines, 25 May.
Allied held territory, 28 May.

2 SITUATION 29/31 MAY

Bray-Dunes   5   4   Nieuport
DUNKIRK   La Panne   3
44, 18, 42, 2   50   Furnes
1
Bergues

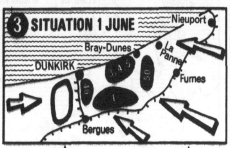

3 SITUATION 1 JUNE

Nieuport
Bray-Dunes   La Panne
DUNKIRK   3, 4, 5
50   Furnes
1
Bergues

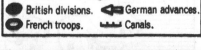

KEY
British divisions.   German advances.
French troops.   Canals.

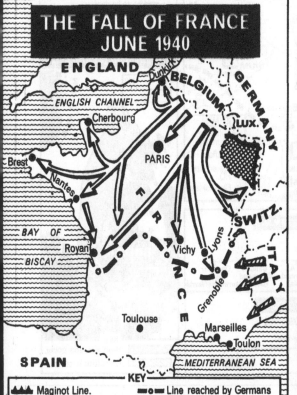

THE FALL OF FRANCE JUNE 1940

ENGLAND
ENGLISH CHANNEL   Dunkirk
BELGIUM   GERMANY
Cherbourg   LUX.
Brest
Nantes   PARIS
BAY OF   F R A N C E   SWITZ.
BISCAY   Royan   Vichy   Lyons   ITALY
Grenoble
Toulouse
Marseilles
Toulon
SPAIN   MEDITERRANEAN SEA

KEY
Maginot Line.   Line reached by Germans
German advances.   at the armistice (22 June).
Italian attacks (20 June).   Trapped French troops.

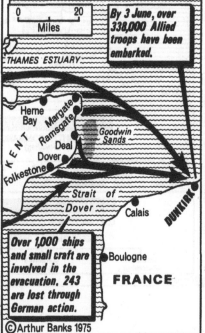

Operation "DYNAMO"

0   20
Miles

By 3 June, over 338,000 Allied troops have been embarked.

THAMES ESTUARY
Herne Bay   Margate
Ramsgate   Goodwin Sands
K E N T   Deal
Folkestone   Dover
Strait of Dover   Calais   DUNKIRK
Boulogne
FRANCE

Over 1,000 ships and small craft are involved in the evacuation. 243 are lost through German action.

© Arthur Banks 1975

THE BATTLE OF BRITAIN 1940

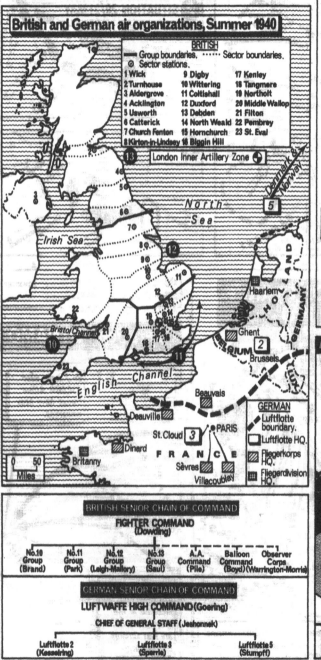

British and German air organizations, Summer 1940

BRITISH

— Group boundaries. ······ Sector boundaries.
⊙ Sector stations.

1 Wick	9 Digby	17 Kenley
2 Turnhouse	10 Wittering	18 Tangmere
3 Aldergrove	11 Coltishall	19 Northolt
4 Acklington	12 Duxford	20 Middle Wallop
5 Usworth	13 Debden	21 Filton
6 Catterick	14 North Weald	22 Pembrey
7 Church Fenton	15 Hornchurch	23 St. Eval
8 Kirton-in-Lindsey	16 Biggin Hill	

London Inner Artillery Zone

North Sea

Eirish Sea

Denmark & Norway

5

Haarlem

HOLLAND

GERMANY

Ghent

2

Brussels

BELGIUM

English Channel

Bristol Channel

10

Beauvais

Deauville

St.Cloud 3 PARIS

Dinard

FRANCE

Sèvres

Villacoublay

Britanny

0 50 Miles

GERMAN
— Luftflotte boundary.
☐ Luftflotte HQ.
▨ Fliegerkorps HQ.
▦ Fliegerdivision HQ.

BRITISH SENIOR CHAIN OF COMMAND

FIGHTER COMMAND
(Dowding)

| No.10 Group (Brand) | No.11 Group (Park) | No.12 Group (Leigh-Mallory) | No.13 Group (Saul) | A.A. Command (Pile) | Balloon Command (Boyd) | Observer Corps (Warrington-Morris) |

GERMAN SENIOR CHAIN OF COMMAND

LUFTWAFFE HIGH COMMAND (Goering)

CHIEF OF GENERAL STAFF (Jeschonnek)

| Luftflotte 2 (Kesselring) | Luftflotte 3 (Sperrle) | Luftflotte 5 (Stumpff) |

© Arthur Banks 1975

GERMAN OFFENSIVE PLANS

1. RECONNAISSANCE
Initial phase for Luftwaffe to probe R.A.F. defences, and gain general knowledge of the unfamiliar airspace.

2. BATTLE WITH R.A.F.
This phase to be a "direct clash" fight to eliminate Fighter Command and its airfields.

3. DESTRUCTION OF BRITAIN'S WAR ECONOMY
An offensive against urban centres in general and London in particular.

BRITISH DEFENSIVE PLANS

1. R.A.F. Fighter Command to concentrate on the destruction of enemy bombers; "fighter only" clashes to be avoided.
2. Protection of airfields and the important radiolocation sites.

BRITISH RADIOLOCATION NET

0 200 Miles

NORWAY

BRITAIN

HOLLAND

BELGIA

FRANCE

KEY
▓ High altitude cover.
▨ Low altitude cover.

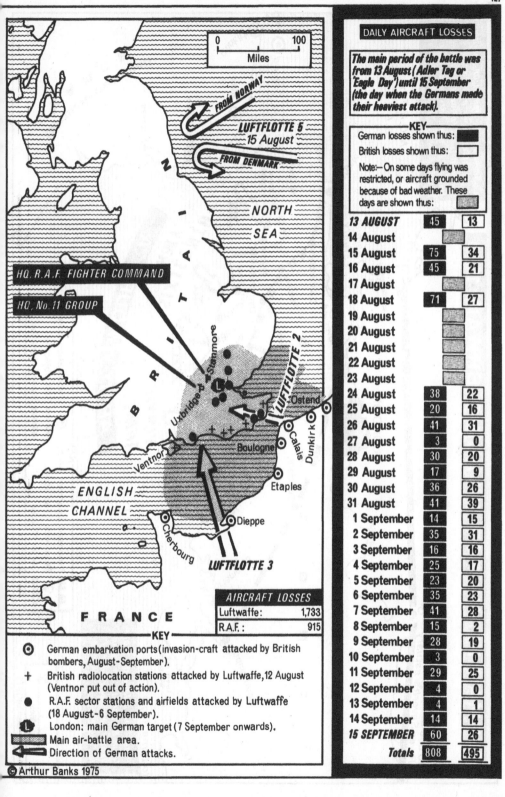

GERMAN PLANS FOR INVADING BRITAIN 1940

Code-named Operation Sealion these plans were postponed indefinitely following Luftwaffe's failure to gain air-mastery over England in the Battle of Britain.

Plans for a landing front from Ramsgate to Lyme Regis were considered but discounted.

KEY

- ▲▲▲ Proposed lodgment area.
- ⓞ Embarkation ports.
- ⌂ Paratroop drop zone.
- - - First objective.
- ⇨ Corps attacks.
- ▬▬ Second objective.

0 — 20 Miles

© Arthur Banks 1975

to line of the River Severn's estuary

to Lyme Regis

NORTH SEA

ENGLAND

LONDON

Thames Estuary

Thames

ENGLISH CHANNEL

Strait of Dover

German-occupied FRANCE

ARMY GROUP "A"

SIXTEENTH ARMY

NINTH ARMY

Isle of Wight

Oxford · Maldon · Gravesend · Guildford · Southampton · Portsmouth · Bognor Regis · Worthing · Brighton · Newhaven · Eastbourne · Bexhill · Hastings · Rye · Uckfield · Etchingham · Tenterden · Dymchurch · Hythe · Ashford · Canterbury · Folkestone · Dover · Deal · Ramsgate · Margate

Dunkirk · to Ostend · Calais · Boulogne · Etaples · Dieppe

XIII · VII · XXXVIII · VIII

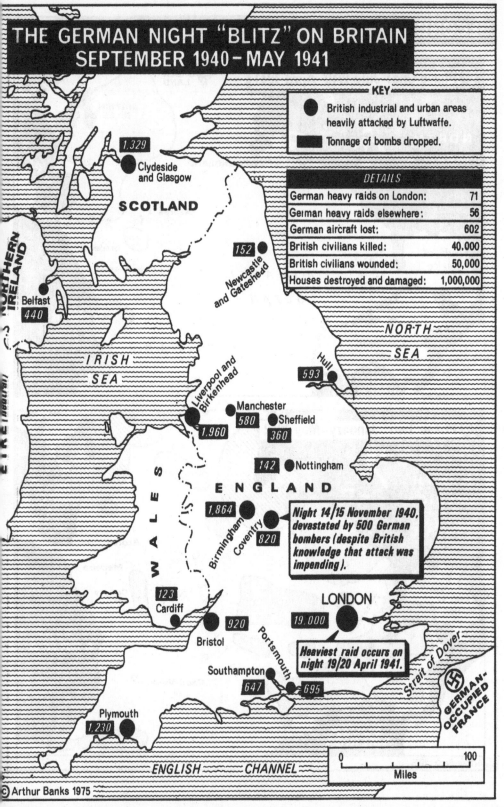

THE GERMAN NIGHT "BLITZ" ON BRITAIN
SEPTEMBER 1940 – MAY 1941

KEY

● British industrial and urban areas heavily attacked by Luftwaffe.

■ Tonnage of bombs dropped.

DETAILS	
German heavy raids on London:	71
German heavy raids elsewhere:	56
German aircraft lost:	602
British civilians killed:	40,000
British civilians wounded:	50,000
Houses destroyed and damaged:	1,000,000

1,329 Clydeside and Glasgow

SCOTLAND

NORTHERN IRELAND

Belfast 440

152 Newcastle and Gateshead

NORTH SEA

IRISH SEA

Liverpool and Birkenhead 1,960

Hull 593

Manchester 580

Sheffield 360

142 ● Nottingham

E N G L A N D

W A L E S

1,864 Birmingham

Coventry 820

Night 14/15 November 1940, devastated by 500 German bombers (despite British knowledge that attack was impending).

123 Cardiff

920 Bristol

LONDON 19,000

Portsmouth

Heaviest raid occurs on night 19/20 April 1941.

Strait of Dover

GERMAN-OCCUPIED FRANCE

Southampton 647

695

Plymouth 1,230

ENGLISH — CHANNEL

0 — 100
Miles

© Arthur Banks 1975

SECOND BATTLE OF THE ATLANTIC

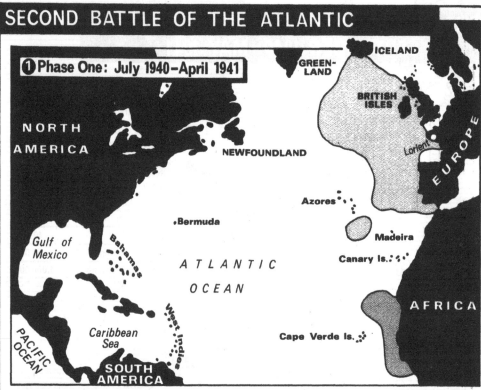

1 Phase One: July 1940–April 1941

ICELAND
GREEN-LAND
BRITISH ISLES
NORTH AMERICA
NEWFOUNDLAND
EUROPE
Lorient
Azores
.Bermuda
Madeira
Gulf of Mexico
Bahamas
Canary Is.
ATLANTIC OCEAN
AFRICA
West Indies
Caribbean Sea
PACIFIC OCEAN
Cape Verde Is.
SOUTH AMERICA

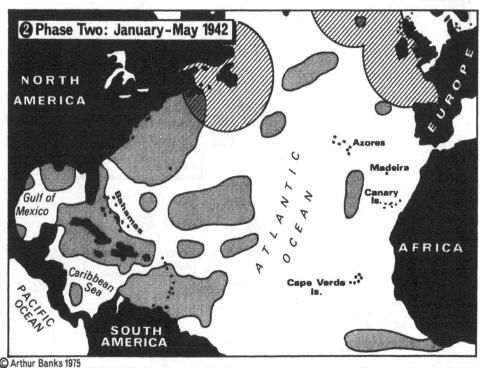

2 Phase Two: January–May 1942

NORTH AMERICA
EUROPE
Azores
Madeira
Canary Is.
Gulf of Mexico
Bahamas
ATLANTIC OCEAN
AFRICA
Caribbean Sea
PACIFIC OCEAN
Cape Verde Is.
SOUTH AMERICA

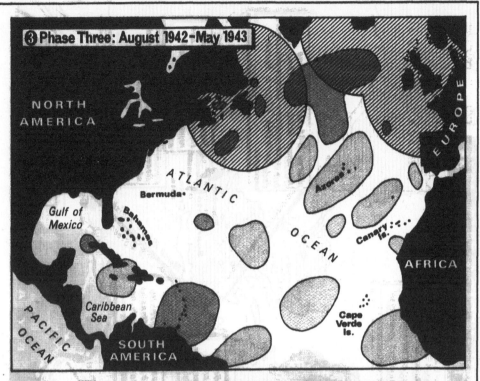

KEY

Areas where German U-boats sank large numbers of Allied and neutral ships.

Ranges of Allied land-based air cover.

Lorient. First German U-boat base on Atlantic coast (operational from July 1940).

Allied convoy routes.

Allied bases.

These map sections illustrate phases of the naval fight in the vital north Atlantic theatre. The German assault against Allied merchant shipping was three-pronged: via U-boats, surface raiders and long-range aircraft. 1,163 U-boats were involved (often in pack formations) of which 784 were sunk. Allied (plus neutral) losses totalled 2,826 ships (a tonnage of 14,680,000).

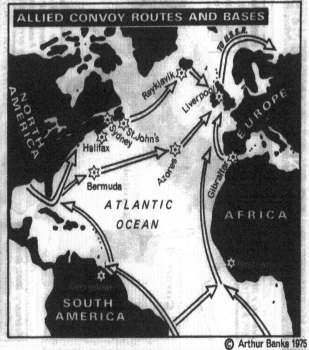

© Arthur Banks 1975

THE MEDITERRANEAN AND NORTH AFRICA 1940–1941

KEY

- Italian-held territory.
- British advances.
- ✕ Important naval clash.
- ✕ Important tank clash.

BLACK SEA

March 1941, battle off Cape Matapan: British sink three Italian cruisers and two Italian destroyers, but battleship "Vittorio Veneto" escapes.

September 1940, British fleet attacks targets and repels Italian E-boat sortie.

December 1941, Italian-manned slow-speed torpedoes ("pigs") incapacitate two British battleships in harbour.

March 1941, German aircraft drop acoustic and magnetic mines in Suez Canal, closing it for three weeks.

Alexandria

E G Y P T

Sidi Barrani

Rhodes

Scarpanto

Crete

Aegean Sea

March 1941, British troops to Greece

Tobruk

Derna

Benghazi

El Aghella

L I B Y A

ALBANIA

Adriatic Sea

ITALY

Taranto

Sardinia

Corsica

Genoa

Sicily

Malta

MEDITERRANEAN SEA

November 1940, British carrier-borne aircraft inflict heavy damage on Italian naval units.

Following hesitant Italian advance into Egypt in September 1940, British launch counter-offensive in December. This develops into full-scale advance and victory: British take 130,000 prisoners.

Tripoli

Castra Benit Airfield

TUNISIA

February 1941, bombarded by British Force "H" (from Gibraltar).

February 1941, British 'U'-class submarines commence operations against Axis shipping plying between Italy and Libya.

February 1941, Rommel arrives here to command German Afrika Korps in Libya.

0   200
Miles

© Arthur Banks 1975

BRITISH NAVAL LOSSES OFF GREECE AND CRETE 1941
0
200
Miles
KEY
British warships sunk or badly damaged.
British transports " " " " .
GREECE
TURKEY
Rhodes
Scarpanto
CRETE
26 May, H.M.S. "Formidable" (sole British aircraft-carrier in area dominated by 500 Axis aircraft) is dive-bombed and put out of action.
MEDITERRANEAN
SEA
THE TOLL
Warships sunk: 9
Warships seriously damaged: 7
Warships damaged: 6
NORTH AFRICA

© Arthur Banks 1975

ROMMEL IN NORTH AFRICA 1941–1942
1 His advance.
2 His retreat.
3 His second advance.
1
Derna
Benghazi
HIGH LAND
Mechili
Tobruk
Bardia
Buq Buq
Msus
Besieged but not overrun.
Halfaya Pass
El Agheila
Agedabia
LIBYA
EGYPT
0
200
Miles
KEY
German advance.
British lines.
MARCH – MAY 1941
2
Derna
Tobruk
Benghazi
HIGH LAND
Mechili
Bardia
Sidi Rezegh
Msus
Relieved by British on 7 December.
El Agheila
Agedabia
LIBYA
EGYPT
0
200
Miles
KEY
British advance.
Tank clash.
NOVEMBER – DECEMBER 1941
3
Gazala
Cauldron
Knightsbridge
Benghazi
Mersa Matruh
El Alamein
February – June : stalemate situation.
ALAM HALFA
Qattara Depression
El Agheila
0
300
Miles
KEY
German advance.
Battle / positions.
JANUARY – JULY 1942

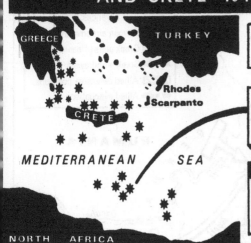

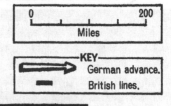

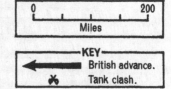

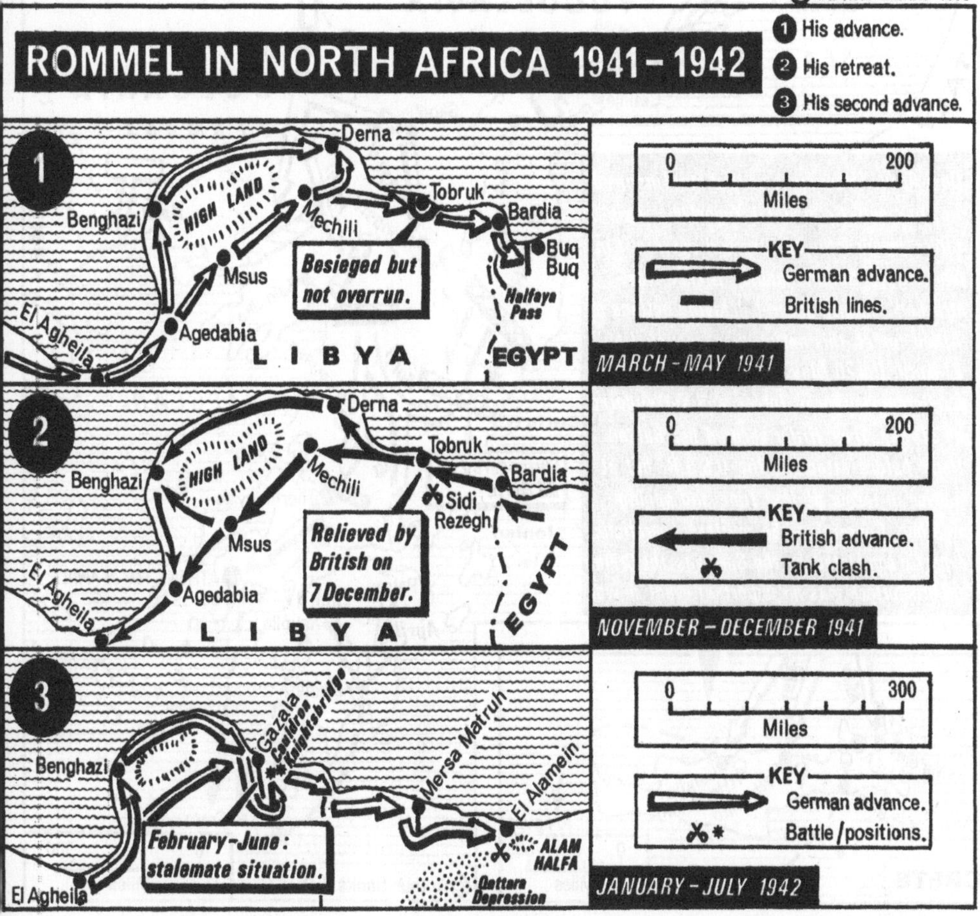

SECURING THE BALKAN FLANK SPRING 1941

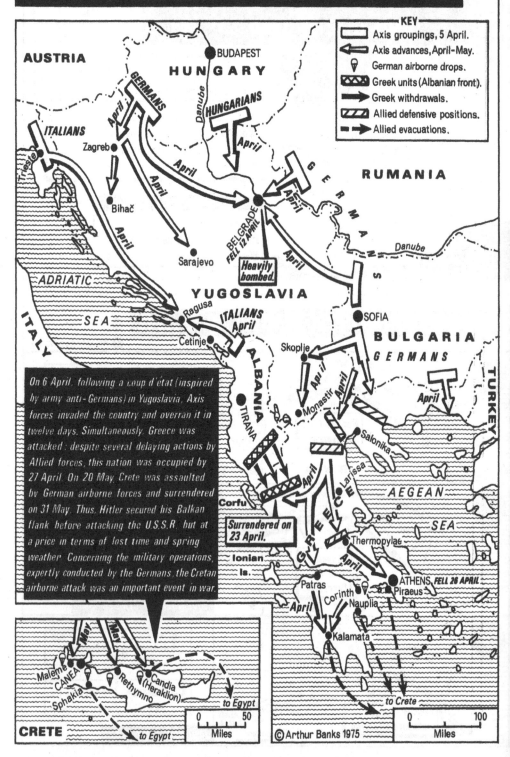

KEY

- Axis groupings, 5 April.
- Axis advances, April–May.
- German airborne drops.
- Greek units (Albanian front).
- Greek withdrawals.
- Allied defensive positions.
- Allied evacuations.

AUSTRIA

BUDAPEST

HUNGARY

GERMANS

April

ITALIANS

April

Zagreb

HUNGARIANS

April

Danube

April

Bihač

RUMANIA

GERMANS

Sarajevo

BELGRADE
FELL 12 APRIL

April

Heavily bombed.

Danube

ADRIATIC

YUGOSLAVIA

SEA

Ragusa

ITALIANS
April

SOFIA

ITALY

Cetinje

ALBANIA

Skoplje

BULGARIA

GERMANS

April

On 6 April, following a coup d'état (inspired by army anti-Germans) in Yugoslavia, Axis forces invaded the country and overran it in twelve days. Simultaneously, Greece was attacked: despite several delaying actions by Allied forces, this nation was occupied by 27 April. On 20 May, Crete was assaulted by German airborne forces and surrendered on 31 May. Thus, Hitler secured his Balkan flank before attacking the U.S.S.R. but at a price in terms of lost time and spring weather. Concerning the military operations, expertly conducted by the Germans, the Cretan airborne attack was an important event in war.

TIRANA

Monastir

April

Salonika

April

Larissa

Corfu

AEGEAN

Surrendered on 23 April.

SEA

Ionian Is.

GREECE

Thermopylae

April

ATHENS, FELL 26 APRIL

Patras

Corinth

Nauplia

Piraeus

April

Kalamata

TURKEY

to Crete

CRETE

May

May

May

Maleme

CANEA

Rethymno

Candia
(Heraklion)

Sphakia

to Egypt

to Egypt

0   50
Miles

to Crete

© Arthur Banks 1975

0   100
Miles

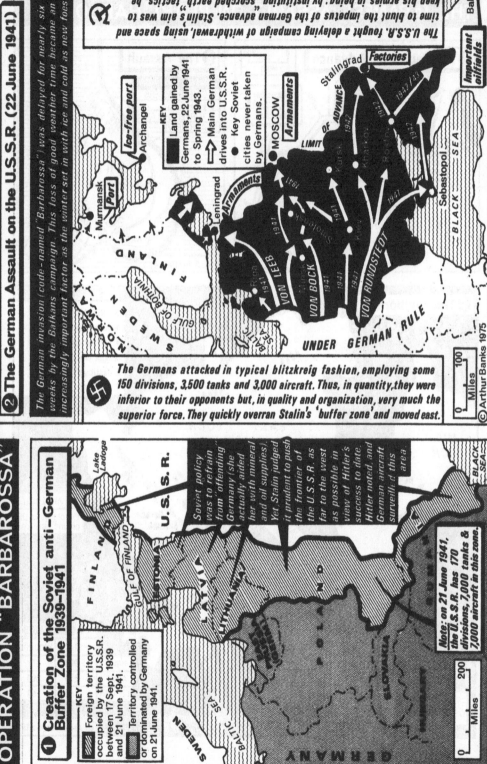

2 The German Assault on the U.S.S.R. (22 June 1941)

The German invasion (code-named "Barbarossa") was delayed for nearly six weeks by the Balkans campaign. This loss of good weather time became an increasingly important factor as the winter set in with ice and cold as new foes.

The U.S.S.R. fought a delaying campaign of withdrawal, using space and time to blunt the impetus of the German advance. Stalin's aim was to "keep his armies in being; by instituting "scorched earth" tactics, he denied Soviet crops and resources to the invaders.

KEY
- Land gained by Germans, 22 June 1941 to Spring 1943.
- Main German drives into U.S.S.R.
- Key Soviet cities never taken by Germans.

Ice-free port Archangel — *Port* Murmansk — Leningrad — MOSCOW — Armaments — Stalingrad — *Factories* — Armaments — Sebastopol — BLACK SEA — Baku — *Important oilfields*

UNDER GERMAN RULE

VON LEEB — VON BOCK — VON RUNDSTEDT — LIMIT OF ADVANCE — Riga — Minsk — Smolensk — Kiev — Kharkov — Kursk — Rostov

FINLAND — NORWAY — SWEDEN — GULF OF BOTHNIA — BALTIC SEA

The Germans attacked in typical blitzkreig fashion, employing some 150 divisions, 3,500 tanks and 3,000 aircraft. Thus, in quantity, they were inferior to their opponents but, in quality and organization, very much the superior force. They quickly overran Stalin's 'buffer zone' and moved east.

0   100   Miles   © Arthur Banks 1975

OPERATION "BARBAROSSA"

1 Creation of the Soviet anti-German Buffer Zone 1939-1941

KEY
- Foreign territory occupied by the U.S.S.R. between 17 Sept. 1939 and 21 June 1941.
- Territory controlled or dominated by Germany on 21 June 1941.

Soviet policy was to refrain from "offending" Germany (she actually aided her with minerals and oil supplies). Yet Stalin judged it prudent to push the frontier of the U.S.S.R. as far to the west as possible in view of Hitler's success to date. Hitler noted, and German aircraft surveilled this area.

Note: on 21 June 1941, the U.S.S.R. has 170 divisions, 7,000 tanks & 7,000 aircraft in this zone.

Lake Ledoga — U.S.S.R. — FINLAND — GULF OF FINLAND — ESTONIA — LATVIA — LITHUANIA — POLAND — GERMANY — SLOVAKIA — RUMANIA — BLACK SEA — BALTIC SEA — SWEDEN

0   200   Miles

THE JAPANESE ASSAULT ON PEARL HARBOR 1941

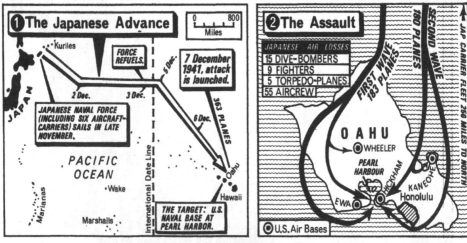

1 The Japanese Advance

0 800 Miles

Kuriles

FORCE REFUELS.

7 December 1941, attack is launched.

JAPAN

2 Dec. 3 Dec.

5 Dec.

6 Dec.

363 PLANES

JAPANESE NAVAL FORCE (INCLUDING SIX AIRCRAFT-CARRIERS) SAILS IN LATE NOVEMBER.

PACIFIC OCEAN

•Wake

Oahu

Hawaii

Marianas

Marshalls

International Date Line

THE TARGET: U.S. NAVAL BASE AT PEARL HARBOR.

2 The Assault

JAPANESE AIR LOSSES
| 15 DIVE-BOMBERS |
| 9 FIGHTERS |
| 5 TORPEDO-PLANES |
| 55 AIRCREW |

180 PLANES

SECOND WAVE

FIRST WAVE 183 PLANES

JAP. CARRIER FLEET 260 MILES TO NORTH

O A H U

WHEELER

PEARL HARBOUR

HICKHAM

KANEOHE

EWA

Honolulu

⊙ U.S. Air Bases

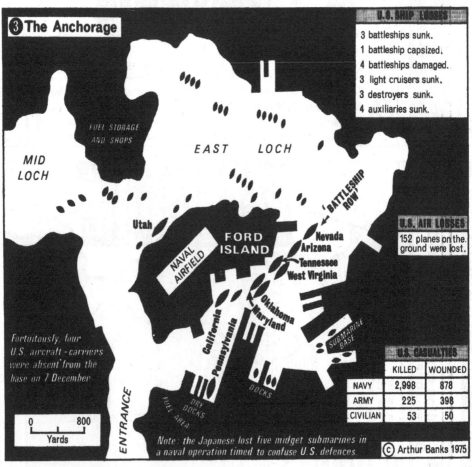

3 The Anchorage

U.S. SHIP LOSSES

3 battleships sunk.
1 battleship capsized.
4 battleships damaged.
3 light cruisers sunk.
3 destroyers sunk.
4 auxiliaries sunk.

FUEL STORAGE AND SHOPS

EAST LOCH

MID LOCH

'BATTLESHIP ROW'

Utah

FORD ISLAND

NAVAL AIRFIELD

Nevada
Arizona
Tennessee
West Virginia

U.S. AIR LOSSES

152 planes on the ground were lost.

Oklahoma
Maryland

California
Pennsylvania

SUBMARINE BASE

Fortuitously, four U.S. aircraft-carriers were absent from the base on 7 December.

DOCKS

DRY DOCKS

FUEL AREA

ENTRANCE

0 800 Yards

U.S. CASUALTIES

	KILLED	WOUNDED
NAVY	2,998	878
ARMY	225	398
CIVILIAN	53	50

Note: The Japanese lost five midget submarines in a naval operation timed to confuse U.S. defences.

© Arthur Banks 1975

JAPANESE CONQUESTS 1941–1942

1000 Miles

U.S.A.

Dutch Harbor
Aleutian Is.
Kiska
Attu

U.S.S.R.
SAKHALIN
Kurile Is.
HOKKAIDO
Tokyo
HONSHU
SHIKOKU
KYUSHU
Ryukyu Is.
Formosa
Iwojima

PACIFIC OCEAN
June 1942
Midway I.
Hawaiian Is.
Pearl Harbor

Wake I.
Marshall Is.
Guam
Caroline Is.

May 1942
Coral Sea
NEW GUINEA
AUSTRALIA

U.S.S.R.
MONGOLIA
Manchuria
CHINA
Chungking
TIBET
INDIA
BURMA
THAI-LAND
FR. INDO-CHINA
Hainan
MALAYA
Singapore
Sumatra
Borneo
Celebes
Java
DUTCH EAST INDIES
PHILIPPINE IS.
Manila
Feb. 1942
Jan. 1942
Dec. 1941

KEY

The Japanese Empire on the eve of its attack on Pearl Harbor in December 1941.

Japanese strikes, Dec. 1941.

Greatest extent of Japanese conquests (January 1943).

Important naval/air clashes.

© Arthur Banks 1975

137

THE JAPANESE ASSAULT ON BURMA 1942

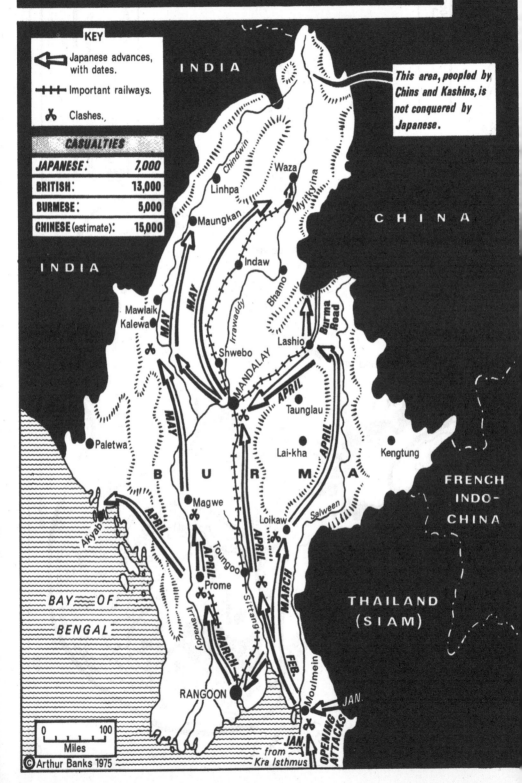

KEY

⬅ Japanese advances, with dates.

╋╋╋ Important railways.

✂ Clashes.

CASUALTIES	
JAPANESE:	7,000
BRITISH:	13,000
BURMESE:	5,000
CHINESE (estimate):	15,000

INDIA

This area, peopled by Chins and Kashins, is not conquered by Japanese.

CHINA

INDIA

Waza

Linhpa

Myitkyina

Maungkan

Indaw

Bhamo

Mawlaik
Kalewa

Shwebo

Lashio

Burma Road

Chindwin

Irrawaddy

MANDALAY

APRIL

Taunglau

Paletwa

Lai-kha

Kengtung

B   U   R   M   A

FRENCH
INDO-
CHINA

Magwe

Loikaw

Salween

MAY

APRIL

Akyab

BAY — OF —

BENGAL

Toungoo

Prome

APRIL

Irrawaddy

Sittang

MARCH

MARCH

THAILAND
(SIAM)

FEB.

Moulmein

JAN.

RANGOON

JAN.
from
Kra Isthmus

OPENING
ATTACKS

0   100
Miles

© Arthur Banks 1975

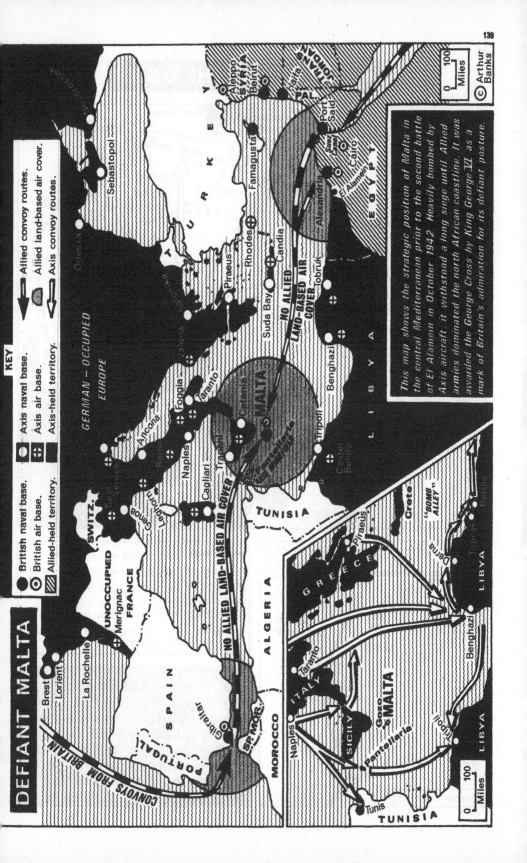

DEFIANT MALTA

This map shows the strategic position of Malta in the central Mediterranean prior to the second battle of El Alamein in October 1942. Heavily bombed by Axis aircraft, it withstood a long siege until Allied armies dominated the north African coastline. It was awarded the George Cross by King George VI as a mark of Britain's admiration for its defiant posture.

KEY

- ● British naval base.
- ◉ British air base.
- ▨ Allied-held territory.
- ◉ Axis naval base.
- ⊕ Axis air base.
- ■ Axis-held territory.
- ← Allied convoy routes.
- ▨ Allied land-based air cover.
- ⇦ Axis convoy routes.

© Arthur Banks

CONVOYS FROM BRITAIN

GERMAN – OCCUPIED EUROPE

UNOCCUPIED FRANCE

Merignac

Brest

Lorient

La Rochelle

SPAIN

PORTUGAL

Gibraltar

SP. MOR.

MOROCCO

ALGERIA

TUNISIA

SWITZ.

Turin

Genoa

Leghorn

Venice

Rome

Naples

Cagliari

Trapani

MALTA

Foggia

Taranto

Ancona

Castel Benito

Tripoli

LIBYA

Benghazi

Tobruk

NO ALLIED LAND-BASED AIR COVER

Suda Bay

Candia

Rhodes

Piraeus

Salonika

TURKEY

Odessa

Sebastopol

Famagusta

Aleppo

Beirut

SYRIA

PAL.

TRANS JORDAN

Port Said

Cairo

El Alamein

Alexandria

EGYPT

NO ALLIED LAND-BASED AIR COVER

GREECE

Piraeus

Crete

"BOMB ALLEY"

Derna

Tobruk

Bardia

Benghazi

LIBYA

ITALY

Naples

Taranto

SICILY

Gozo

MALTA

Pantellaria

Tunis

TUNISIA

0   100   Miles

0   100   Miles

ALLIED AID TO THE U.S.S.R.

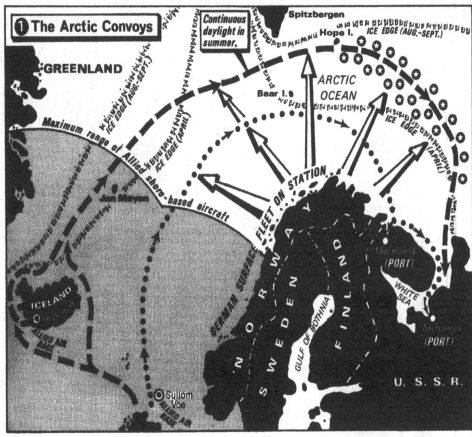

1 The Arctic Convoys

GREENLAND

Continuous daylight in summer.

Spitzbergen

Hope I.

ICE EDGE (AUG.-SEPT.)

Bear I.

ARCTIC OCEAN

ICE EDGE (AUG.-SEPT.)

ICE EDGE (APRIL)

ICE EDGE (APRIL)

Maximum range of Allied shore-based aircraft

FLEET ON STATION

GERMAN SURFACE

ICELAND

N O R W A Y

S W E D E N

F I N L A N D

GULF OF BOTHNIA

Murmansk (PORT)

WHITE SEA

Archangel (PORT)

U.S.S.R.

Sullom Voe

2 The Caspian Route

0   300
Miles

GERMAN LAND THREAT

Astrakhan

Black Sea

U.S.S.R.
CASPIAN SEA

U.S.S.R.

Baku

Tehran

ALLIED AID

PERSIA (IRAN)

I R A Q

Basra

Persian Gulf

© Arthur Banks 1975

KEY

➤ (thick dashed)	Tracks of Allied summer convoys.
➤ (dotted)	Tracks of Allied winter convoys.
▨ (shaded area)	Area overflown by Allied land-based aircraft.
⇨ (open arrow)	German air and U-boat attacks.
✪ ✪ ✪	Area where convoy PQ 17 was massacred after scattering in July 1942.

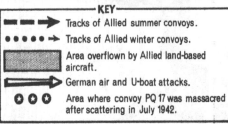

Anglo-American aid to the U.S.S.R. equalled about 5% of Soviet internal production. It included over 20,000 aircraft, 13,000 tanks, food, clothing, medical supplies, petroleum, and electronic equipment. It went via two main routes (see maps). 40 Allied convoys made the northern journey despite German interference in transit (815 merchant ships sailed; 98 were sunk). The Caspian route, although safer, was indirect from the west

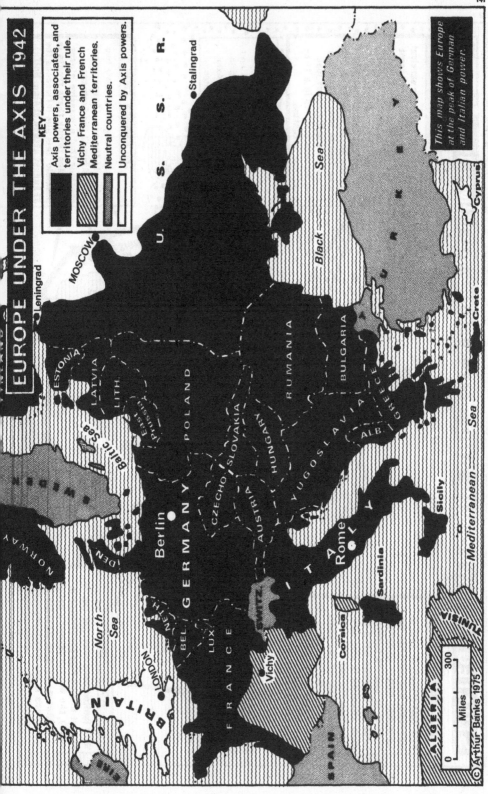

EUROPE UNDER THE AXIS 1942

KEY

- Axis powers, associates, and territories under their rule.
- Vichy France and French Mediterranean territories.
- Neutral countries.
- Unconquered by Axis powers.

This map shows Europe at the peak of German and Italian power.

© Arthur Banks 1975

Miles

0   300

U. S. S. R.

Stalingrad

Leningrad

MOSCOW

Black Sea

TURKEY

Cyprus

ESTONIA

LATVIA

LITH.

PRUSSIA

Baltic Sea

POLAND

RUMANIA

BULGARIA

GREECE

Crete

CZECHO-SLOVAKIA

HUNGARY

YUGOSLAVIA

ALB.

AUSTRIA

SWEDEN

NORWAY

North Sea

DEN.

Berlin

GERMANY

NETH.

BEL.

LUX.

FRANCE

Vichy

SWITZ.

ITALY

Rome

Corsica

Sardinia

Sicily

Mediterranean Sea

LONDON

BRITAIN

SPAIN

ALGERIA

TUNISIA

FINLAND

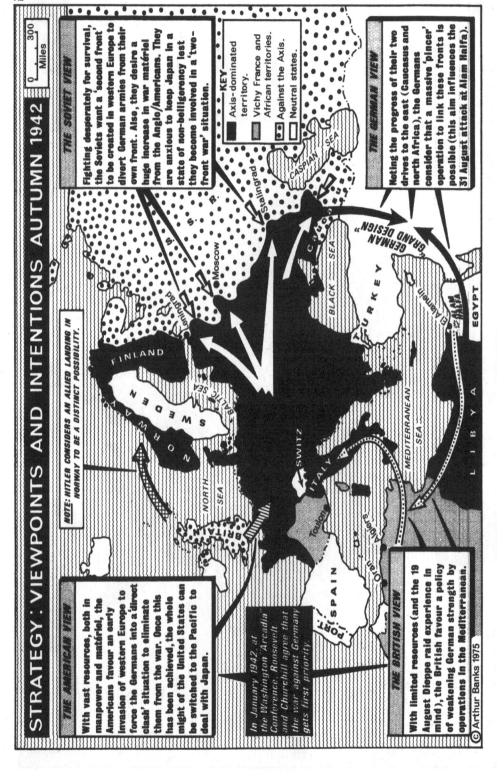

STRATEGY: VIEWPOINTS AND INTENTIONS AUTUMN 1942

0 — 300 Miles

THE SOVIET VIEW

Fighting desperately for survival, the Soviets want a 'second front' to be created in western Europe to divert German armies from their own front. Also, they desire a huge increase in war matériel from the Anglo/Americans. They are anxious to keep Japan in a state of non-belligerency lest they become involved in a 'two-front war' situation.

KEY

◼ Axis–dominated territory.

▦ Vichy France and African territories.

⊡ Against the Axis.

☐ Neutral states.

THE GERMAN VIEW

Noting the progress of their two drives to the east (Caucasus and north Africa), the Germans consider that a massive 'pincer' operation to link these fronts is possible (this aim influences the 31 August attack at Alam Halfa).

NOTE: HITLER CONSIDERS AN ALLIED LANDING IN NORWAY TO BE A DISTINCT POSSIBILITY.

GERMAN "GRAND DESIGN"

U.S.S.R.

CASPIAN SEA

Stalingrad

Moscow

Leningrad

FINLAND

NORWAY

SWEDEN

BALTIC SEA

NORTH SEA

BRITAIN

CAUCASUS

BLACK SEA

TURKEY

SWITZ.

ITALY

MEDITERRANEAN SEA

Toulon

Algiers

Oran

SPAIN

PORT.

El Alamein

ALAM HALFA

EGYPT

L I B Y A

THE AMERICAN VIEW

With vast resources, both in manpower and matériel, the Americans favour an early invasion of western Europe to force the Germans into a 'direct clash' situation to eliminate them from the war. Once this has been achieved, the whole might of the United States can be switched to the Pacific to deal with Japan.

In January 1942, at the Washington 'Arcadia' Conference, Roosevelt and Churchill agree that the war against Germany gets first priority.

THE BRITISH VIEW

With limited resources (and the 19 August Dieppe raid experience in mind), the British favour a policy of weakening German strength by operations in the Mediterranean.

© Arthur Banks 1975

THE GERMAN REBUFF AT ALAM HALFA
31 AUGUST - 2 SEPTEMBER 1942

This battle was decisive: German expansion in the area was ended.

KEY

British minefields.	Axis tank units.
British dummy minefields.	Axis drives.
Axis minefields.	Axis feints.
British divisional defences.	British moves.
Axis divisional defences.	Ridges.
British tank formations.	Tracks.

ARABS' GULF

Sidi Abd el Rahman

KIDNEY RIDGE

164 Div.

XXI CORPS

COASTAL ROAD

9 Australian Div.

El Alamein

26 Bde. Aust.

El Imayid

HQ XXX CORPS

Trento Div.

1 South African Div.

Ramcke Div.

X CORPS

Bologna Div.

5 Indian Div.

RUWEISAT RIDGE

23 Armd. Bde.

22 Armd. Bde.

ALAM HALFA

HQ XIII CORPS

44 Div.

Brescia Div.

QARET EL ABD

2 New Zealand Div.

31 Aug.

10 Armd. Div.

1 Sept.

8 Armd. Bde.

90 Light Div.

31 Aug.

90 Lt. Div.

21 Div.

15 Pz. Div.

XX

7 Motor. Bde.

RAGIL

DAK

MAIN DRIVE

31 Aug.

DAK

4 Armd. Bde.

31 Aug.

31 Aug.

Recce Group

7 Armd. Div.

SAMAKET GABALLA

QARET EL HIMEIMAT

31 Aug.

SCORE SHEET

DETAILS	AXIS	BRITISH
CASUALTIES	2,910	1,640
TANKS LOST	49	68
GUNS LOST	55	18

0 ... 5 Miles

© Arthur Banks 1975

QATTARA DEPRESSION (impassable)

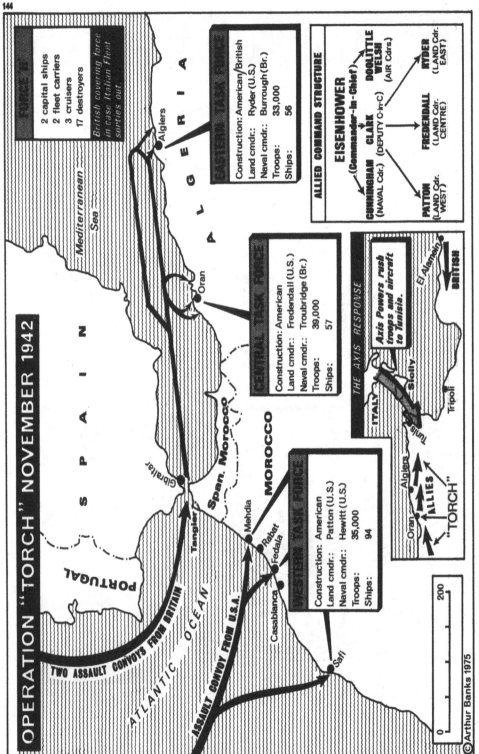

OPERATION "TORCH" NOVEMBER 1942

FORCE "H"

| 2 capital ships |
| 2 fleet carriers |
| 3 cruisers |
| 17 destroyers |

British covering force in case Italian Fleet sorties out

EASTERN TASK FORCE

Construction: American/British
Land cmdr.: Ryder (U.S.)
Naval cmdr.: Burrough (Br.)
Troops: 33,000
Ships: 56

CENTRAL TASK FORCE

Construction: American
Land cmdr.: Fredendall (U.S.)
Naval cmdr.: Troubridge (Br.)
Troops: 39,000
Ships: 57

WESTERN TASK FORCE

Construction: American
Land cmdr.: Patton (U.S.)
Naval cmdr.: Hewitt (U.S.)
Troops: 35,000
Ships: 94

ALLIED COMMAND STRUCTURE

EISENHOWER
(Commander-in-Chief)

CLARK
(DEPUTY C-in-C)

CUNNINGHAM (NAVAL Cdr.)

PATTON (LAND Cdr. WEST)

FREDENDALL (LAND Cdr. CENTRE)

DOOLITTLE WELSH (AIR Cdrs.)

RYDER (LAND Cdr. EAST)

THE AXIS RESPONSE

Axis Powers rush troops and aircraft to Tunisia.

ITALY
Sicily
Tunis
Tripoli
Algiers
Oran
El Alamein
BRITISH

"TORCH"
ALLIES

Mediterranean Sea
ALGERIA
Algiers
Oran
SPAIN
Gibraltar
Tangier
Span. Morocco
Rabat
Mehdia
Fedala
Casablanca
Safi
MOROCCO
PORTUGAL
ATLANTIC OCEAN

TWO ASSAULT CONVOYS FROM BRITAIN
ASSAULT CONVOY FROM U.S.A.

0   200

© Arthur Banks 1975

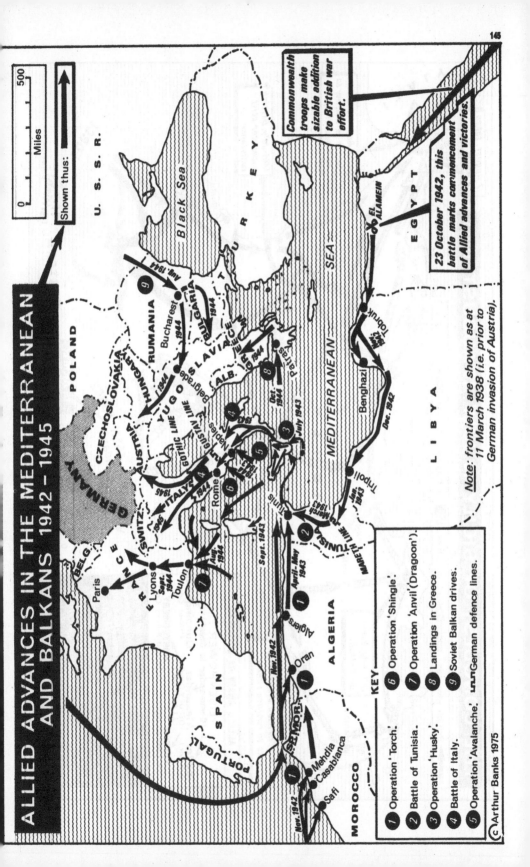

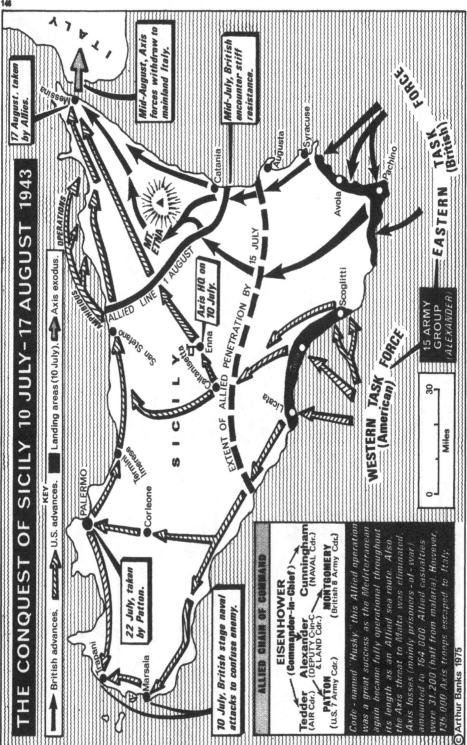

THE CONQUEST OF SICILY 10 JULY–17 AUGUST 1943

ITALY

17 August, taken by Allies.

Mid-August, Axis forces withdraw to mainland Italy.

Mid-July, British encounter stiff resistance.

Messina

Catania

Augusta

Syracuse

Pachino

Avola

EASTERN TASK FORCE (British)

Scoglitti

Gela

Licata

WESTERN TASK FORCE (American)

15 ARMY GROUP (ALEXANDER)

0   30
Miles

MT. ETNA

ALLIED LINE 1 AUGUST

Axis HO on 10 July.

Enna

Caltanissetta

EXTENT OF ALLIED PENETRATION BY 15 JULY

San Stefano

AMPHIBIOUS OPERATIONS

Termini Imerese

PALERMO

Corleone

22 July, taken by Patton.

Trapani

Marsala

10 July, British stage naval attacks to confuse enemy.

S I C I L Y

KEY

British advances. → U.S. advances. ▨▨ British advances. ▣ Landing areas (10 July). ⬆ Axis exodus.

ALLIED CHAIN OF COMMAND

EISENHOWER
(Commander-in-Chief)

Tedder ———— Alexander ———— Cunningham
(AIR Cdr.)   (DEPUTY C-in-C   (NAVAL Cdr.)
             & LAND Cdr.)

PATTON   **MONTGOMERY**
(U.S. 7 Army Cdr.)   (British 8 Army Cdr.)

*Code-named 'Husky' this Allied operation
was a great success as the Mediterranean
again became fully operational throughout
its length as an Allied sea route. Also
the Axis threat to Malta was eliminated.
Axis losses (mainly prisoners-of-war)
amounted to 164,000. Allied casualties
were 31,200 (half from malaria). However,
135,000 Axis troops escaped to Italy.*

© Arthur Banks 1975

146

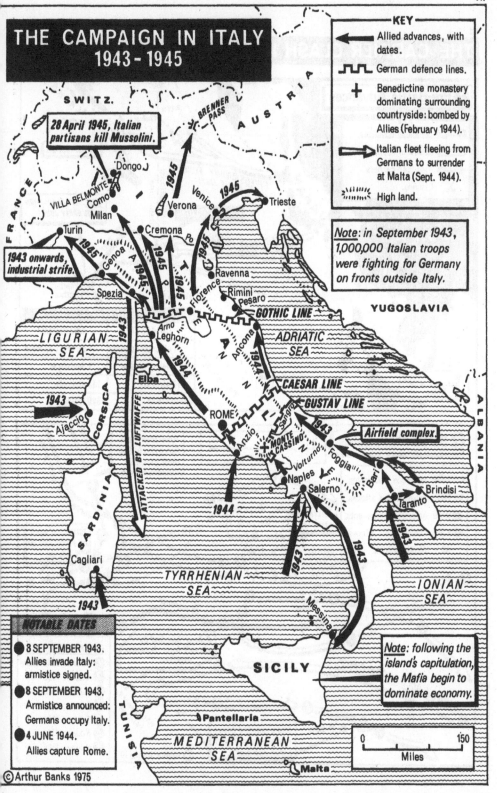

THE CAMPAIGN IN ITALY
1943 - 1945

KEY

← Allied advances, with dates.

⊓⊔ German defence lines.

✚ Benedictine monastery dominating surrounding countryside: bombed by Allies (February 1944).

⇨ Italian fleet fleeing from Germans to surrender at Malta (Sept. 1944).

〰 High land.

Note: in September 1943, 1,000,000 Italian troops were fighting for Germany on fronts outside Italy.

SWITZ.

AUSTRIA

BRENNER PASS

28 April 1945, Italian partisans kill Mussolini.

Dongo

VILLA BELMONTE

Como

Milan

Verona

Venice 1945

Trieste

FRANCE

Turin

Cremona

Po

1945

1943 onwards, industrial strife.

Genoa

A 1945

Spezia

Ravenna

Florence

Rimini

Pesaro

GOTHIC LINE

YUGOSLAVIA

Arno

Leghorn

ADRIATIC SEA

LIGURIAN SEA

Elba

Ancona

1944

CAESAR LINE

1943

1943

Corsica

Ajaccio

ROME

GUSTAV LINE

Sangro

1943

Airfield complex.

ALBANIA

ATTACKED BY LUFTWAFFE

Anzio

MONTE CASSINO

Volturno

Foggia

Bari

Naples

Salerno

Brindisi

Taranto

1943

SARDINIA

Cagliari

1943

TYRRHENIAN SEA

1943

1943

Messina

IONIAN SEA

NOTABLE DATES

● 8 SEPTEMBER 1943. Allies invade Italy: armistice signed.

● 8 SEPTEMBER 1943. Armistice announced: Germans occupy Italy.

● 4 JUNE 1944. Allies capture Rome.

SICILY

Note: following the island's capitulation, the Mafia begin to dominate economy.

Pantellaria

TUNISIA

MEDITERRANEAN SEA

Malta

0 ⊢ 150

Miles

© Arthur Banks 1975

THE CARRIER CLASH IN MID-PACIFIC IN JUNE 1943

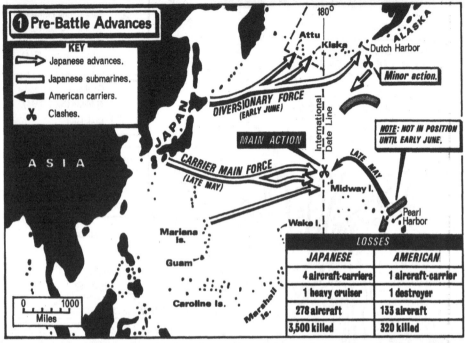

1 Pre-Battle Advances

KEY
- Japanese advances.
- Japanese submarines.
- American carriers.
- Clashes.

ALASKA

Attu Kiska Dutch Harbor

Minor action.

DIVERSIONARY FORCE (EARLY JUNE)

International Date Line

MAIN ACTION

NOTE: NOT IN POSITION UNTIL EARLY JUNE.

LATE MAY

JAPAN

ASIA

CARRIER MAIN FORCE (LATE MAY)

Midway I.

Wake I.

Pearl Harbor

Mariana Is.

Guam

Caroline Is.

Marshall Is.

0 1000
Miles

LOSSES	
JAPANESE	**AMERICAN**
4 aircraft-carriers	1 aircraft-carrier
1 heavy cruiser	1 destroyer
278 aircraft	133 aircraft
3,500 killed	320 killed

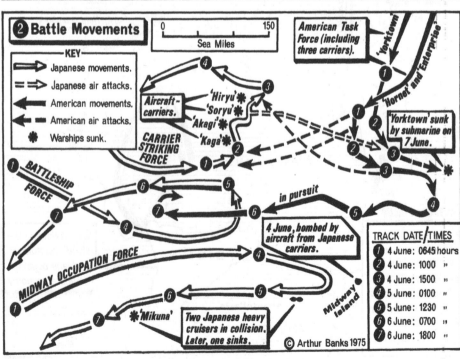

2 Battle Movements

0 150
Sea Miles

American Task Force (including three carriers).

'Yorktown'

'Hornet and Enterprise'

KEY
- Japanese movements.
- Japanese air attacks.
- American movements.
- American air attacks.
- Warships sunk.

Aircraft-carriers.

'Hiryu'
'Soryu'
'Akagi'
'Kaga'

CARRIER STRIKING FORCE

'Yorktown' sunk by submarine on 7 June.

BATTLESHIP FORCE

in pursuit

4 June, bombed by aircraft from Japanese carriers.

MIDWAY OCCUPATION FORCE

Midway Island

'Mikuna'

Two Japanese heavy cruisers in collision. Later, one sinks.

© Arthur Banks 1975

TRACK DATE/TIMES	
1	4 June: 0645 hours
2	4 June: 1000 "
3	4 June: 1500 "
4	5 June: 0100 "
5	5 June: 1230 "
6	6 June: 0700 "
7	6 June: 1800 "

ALLIED ADVANCES IN BURMA 1944-1945

140

KEY

→ Allied advances.

▭ Japanese defensive positions, dated.

✶ Clashes.

┿┿┿ Important railways.

The Japanese were retreating in disorder towards Thailand when the cease-fire came into effect on 15 August 1945.

INDIA

CHINA

SPRING 1944

Waza

Myitkyina

Bhamo

Maungkan

Indaw

INDIA

Mawlaik

Kalewa

WINTER 1944

Irrawaddy

Burma Road

Shwebo

Lashio

Paletwa

B   U   R

Taunglau

MANDALAY

Lai-kha

M   A

Kengtung

Meiktila

1945

Akyab

Magwe

SUMMER

Salween

Loikaw

FRENCH INDO-CHINA

Prome

Toungoo

Sittang

BAY   OF

BENGAL

THAILAND (SIAM)

RANGOON

Moulmein

© Arthur Banks 1975

0   100
Miles

THE LIBERATION OF WESTERN EUROPE 1944

Allied Pre-Invasion Strategy

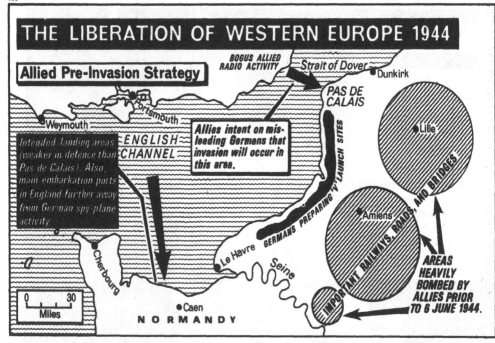

BOGUS ALLIED RADIO ACTIVITY

Strait of Dover • Dunkirk

PAS DE CALAIS

• Lille

Allies intent on misleading Germans that invasion will occur in this area.

Portsmouth

• Weymouth

ENGLISH CHANNEL

Intended landing areas (weaker in defence than Pas de Calais). Also, main embarkation ports in England further away from German spy-plane activity

• Amiens

Cherbourg

Le Havre

GERMANS PREPARING 'V' LAUNCH SITES

Seine

IMPORTANT RAILWAYS, ROADS, AND BRIDGES

AREAS HEAVILY BOMBED BY ALLIES PRIOR TO 6 JUNE 1944.

0 _____ 30
Miles

• Caen

N O R M A N D Y

'Operation Overlord' – the Second Front

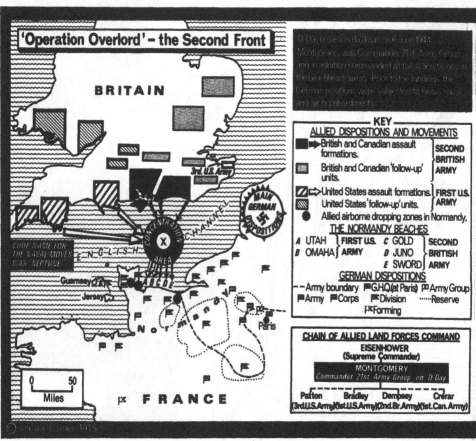

D-Day (invasion day) was 6 June 1944. Montgomery was Commander 21st Army Group and in addition commanded all the Allied troops in the beach-head areas. Prior to the landings, the German positions were subjected to heavy naval and air bombardments.

BRITAIN

3rd. U.S. Army

MAIN GERMAN DISPOSITIONS

CODE NAME FOR THE NAVAL MOVES WAS 'NEPTUNE'

E—N—G—L—I—S—H CHANNEL

CONCENTRATION X AREA

Guernsey

Jersey

A B C D E

N o r m a n d y

• Paris

0 _____ 50
Miles

F R A N C E

KEY

ALLIED DISPOSITIONS AND MOVEMENTS

▶	British and Canadian assault formations.	**SECOND BRITISH ARMY**
▦	British and Canadian 'follow-up' units.	
▨⇨	United States assault formations.	**FIRST U.S. ARMY**
▨	United States 'follow-up' units.	
●	Allied airborne dropping zones in Normandy.	

THE NORMANDY BEACHES

A UTAH	**FIRST U.S.**	C GOLD
B OMAHA	**ARMY**	D JUNO
		E SWORD

SECOND BRITISH ARMY

GERMAN DISPOSITIONS

– Army boundary	⌐G.H.Q. (at Paris)	⌐⌐ Army Group
⌐ Army	⌐ Corps	⌐ Division
		····· Reserve
	⌐× Forming	

CHAIN OF ALLIED LAND FORCES COMMAND

EISENHOWER
(Supreme Commander)

MONTGOMERY
Commander 21st Army Group on D-Day

Patton	Bradley	Dempsey	Crerar
(3rd U.S. Army)	(1st U.S. Army)	(2nd Br. Army)	(1st Can. Army)

© Richard Natkiel 1975

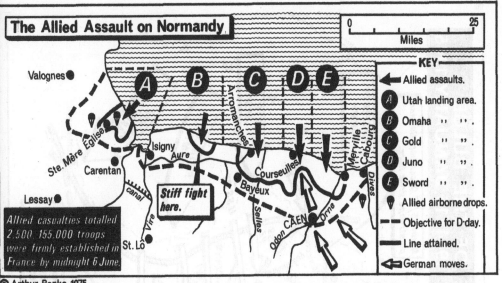

The Allied Assault on Normandy

0 — Miles — 25

KEY
- ← Allied assaults.
- Ⓐ Utah landing area.
- Ⓑ Omaha ,, ,, .
- Ⓒ Gold ,, ,, .
- Ⓓ Juno ,, ,, .
- Ⓔ Sword ,, ,, .
- Allied airborne drops.
- ▬ ▬ ▬ Objective for D-day.
- ▬▬▬ Line attained.
- ⇐ German moves.

Valognes

Ⓐ Ⓑ Ⓒ Ⓓ Ⓔ

Arromanches
Courseulles
Merville
Cabourg
Dives

Ste. Mère Église
Isigny
Aure
Carentan
Bayeux
Selles
CAEN
Odon Orne

Lessay

Stiff fight here.

canal
Vire

Allied casualties totalled 2,500. 155,000 troops were firmly established in France by midnight 6 June.

St. Lô

© Arthur Banks 1975

The Liberation of Northern France and the Low Countries

KEY
- ▬ Allied lodgment area by 31 July 1944.
- → Allied drives 1944/1945.
- Important Allied airborne drop (ending in failure).
- ⋀⋀⋀ German 'West Wall' (Siegfried Line).
- ⟵ German 'V' attack against Britain 1944/1945.
- ▒ Important industrial or mining areas.

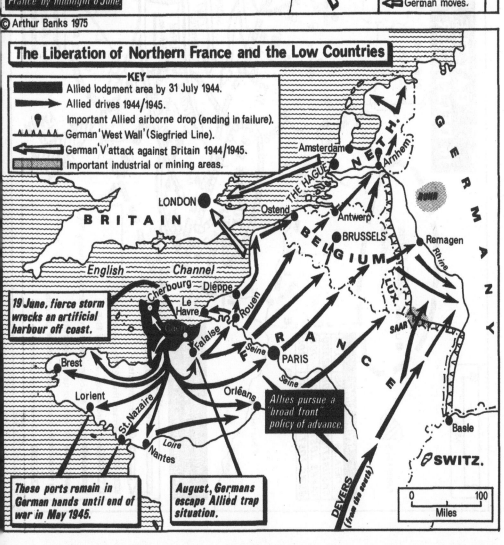

Amsterdam
N E T H.
Arnhem
THE HAGUE
G E R M A N Y
RUHR

LONDON
Ostend
Antwerp
B R I T A I N
BELGIUM
BRUSSELS
Remagen
Rhine

English   Channel

19 June, fierce storm wrecks an artificial harbour off coast.

Cherbourg — Dieppe
Le Havre
Rouen
Caen
Falaise
Seine
PARIS
Seine
F R A N C E
LUX.
SAAR

Allies pursue a "broad front" policy of advance.

Brest
Lorient
St. Nazaire
Orléans
Loire
Nantes

Basle

These ports remain in German hands until end of war in May 1945.

August, Germans escape Allied trap situation.

DEVERS (from the south)

SWITZ.

0 — Miles — 100

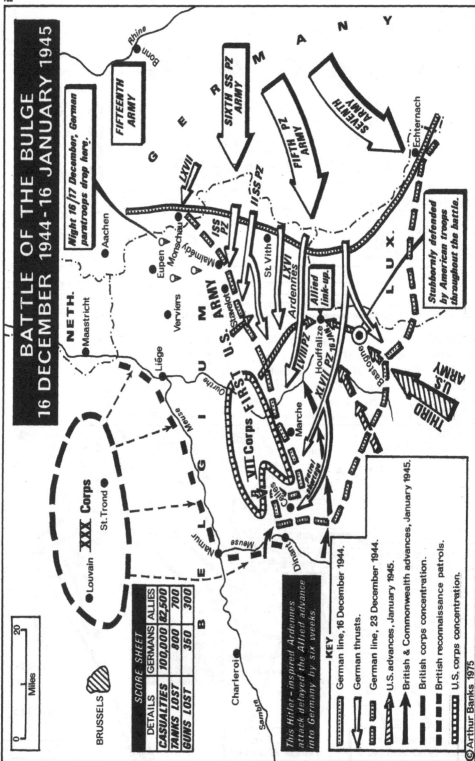

BATTLE OF THE BULGE
16 DECEMBER 1944 - 16 JANUARY 1945

Night 16/17 December, German paratroops drop here.

FIFTEENTH ARMY

G E R M A N Y

SIXTH SS PZ ARMY

FIFTH PZ ARMY

SEVENTH ARMY

Rhine

Bonn

Echternach

LXVII

Aachen

I SS PZ

Monschau

Eupen

Malmedy

II SS PZ

St Vith

LXVI Ardennes

Allied link-up.

Stubbornly defended by American troops throughout the battle.

NETH.

Maastricht

Verviers

Liège

Ourthe

Meuse

U.S. ARMY FIRST

Stavelot

Houffalize

LVIII PZ

XLVII PZ 16 JAN

Bastogne

LUX.

THIRD U.S. ARMY

VII Corps

Marche

Ciney

Meuse

Namur

Dinant

XXX Corps

Louvain

St. Trond

Meuse

Charleroi

Sambre

BRUSSELS

B E L G I U M

This Hitler–inspired Ardennes attack delayed the Allied advance into Germany by six weeks.

0	Miles	20

SCORE SHEET

DETAILS	GERMANS	ALLIES
CASUALTIES	100,000	82,500
TANKS LOST	800	700
GUNS LOST	350	300

KEY

- German line, 16 December 1944.
- German thrusts.
- German line, 23 December 1944.
- U.S. advances, January 1945.
- British & Commonwealth advances, January 1945.
- British corps concentration.
- British reconnaissance patrols.
- U.S. corps concentration.

© Arthur Banks 1975

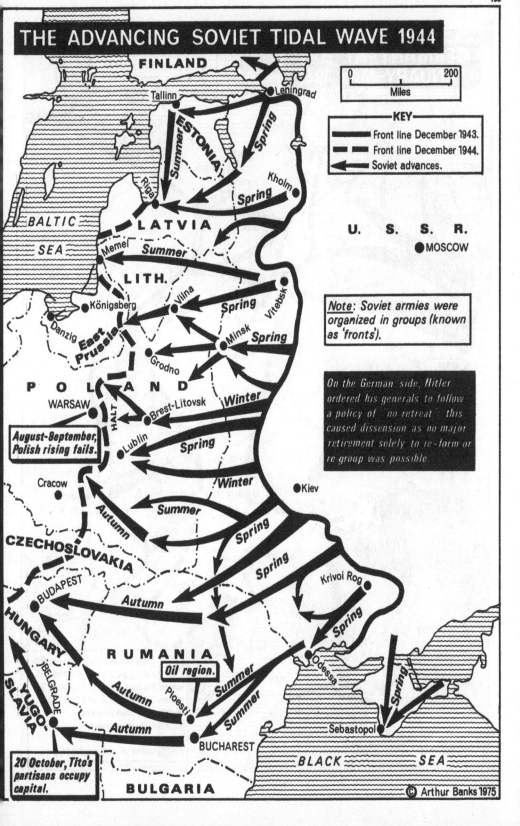

THE ADVANCING SOVIET TIDAL WAVE 1944

FINLAND

Tallinn

Leningrad

ESTONIA

Summer

Spring

Kholm

Riga

Spring

LATVIA

KEY
Front line December 1943.
Front line December 1944.
Soviet advances.

0   200
Miles

BALTIC
SEA

Memel

Summer

LITH.

Königsberg

Vilna

Spring

Vitebsk

Danzig

East
Prussia

Grodno

Minsk

Spring

U.   S.   S.   R.

● MOSCOW

Note: Soviet armies were organized in groups (known as 'fronts').

P O L A N D

WARSAW

HALT

Brest-Litovsk

Winter

August-September, Polish rising fails.

Lublin

Spring

Cracow

Winter

Kiev

Autumn

Summer

On the German side, Hitler ordered his generals to follow a policy of 'no retreat' this caused dissension as no major retirement solely to re-form or re-group was possible.

Spring

CZECHOSLOVAKIA

Spring

Krivoi Rog

BUDAPEST

Autumn

Spring

HUNGARY

BELGRADE

R U M A N I A

Oil region.

Summer

Summer

Odessa

Spring

YUGO-
SLAVIA

Autumn

Ploesti

Summer

Sebastopol

Spring

Autumn

BUCHAREST

20 October, Tito's partisans occupy capital.

BULGARIA

BLACK   SEA

© Arthur Banks 1975

© Arthur Banks 1975

GERMANY AT BAY
JANUARY–MAY 1945

Note: frontiers shown as they were in early 1938 (prior to the German annexation of Austria and the Sudetenland).

DENMARK

SWEDEN

NORTH SEA

BALTIC SEA

Memel

Königsberg

Flensburg

East Prussia

Allenstein

Kiel

Lübeck

Rostock

Kolberg

Danzig

RENDULIC

HIMMLER

Hamburg

Lüneburg

Stettin

ZHUKOV

Bremen

Hanover

Brunswick

Berlin

Frankfurt

Posen

Warsaw

BLASKOWITZ

Arnhem

MONTGOMERY

Magdeburg

ZHUKOV

Lodz

POLAND

BRADLEY

Kassel

Leipzig

Breslau

Cologne

BRADLEY

Erfurt

Dresden

KONIEV

Cracow

BIG. LUX.

GERMANY

Prague

Vistula

MODEL

Frankfurt

CZECHOS

DEVERS

Nuremberg

LOVAKIA

SCHÖRNER

FRANCE

Stuttgart

Danube

PETROV

HAUSSER

Augsburg

Berchtesgaden

Salzburg

Danube

Vienna

MALINOVSKY

Basle

Innsbruck

AUSTRIA

WÖHLER

Budapest

HUNGARY

Berne

TOLBUKHIN

SWITZERLAND

Szeged

Como

Milan

KESSELRING

Trieste

Venice

Zagreb

YUGOSLAVIA

WEICHS

Danube

FRANCE

Turin

Pola

Belgrade

Genoa

CLARK

ADRIATIC

GULF OF GENOA

Florence

SEA

ITALY

0	50	100

Miles

KEY

Allied-held territory, 27 January 1945.

Allied gains, 27 January–8 May 1945.

The battlefronts on 27 January 1945.

The battlefronts on 8 May 1945.

Main Allied advances.

DEVERS Allied commanders.

MODEL German commanders.

Neutral states throughout the war.

ALLIED ADVANCES IN THE PACIFIC 1943–1945

KEY

- The Japanese homeland.
- Broad lines of Allied advances.
- Maximum extent of Japanese conquests.
- Allied penetration by March 1944.
- Allied penetration by March 1945.

JANUARY 1943

Dutch Harbor

Attu

Kiska

HAWAIIAN IS.
Pearl Harbor

Wake

Gilbert Is.

Marshall Is.

NIMITZ

Mariana Is.

Guam

Caroline Is.

MACARTHUR

New Guinea

Rabaul

Guadalcanal

PACIFIC OCEAN

SOVIET THREAT

TOKYO

Hiroshima

Nagasaki

Iwojima

Okinawa

Luzon
PHILIPPINE
ISLANDS
Mindanao

Borneo

Celebes

Java

Sumatra

10 March 1945, U.S. bombers devastate Japanese capital in huge "fire storm" raid. Civilian casualties exceed 180,000.

6 August 1945, U.S. bomber drops atomic (uranium) bomb causing extensive damage and creating radiation hazards. Civilian casualties exceed 148,000.

9 August 1945, U.S. bomber drops atomic (plutonium) bomb. Civilian casualties exceed 65,000.

© Arthur Banks 1975

Miles
0   1000

THE RECONQUEST OF THE PHILIPPINES 1944–1945

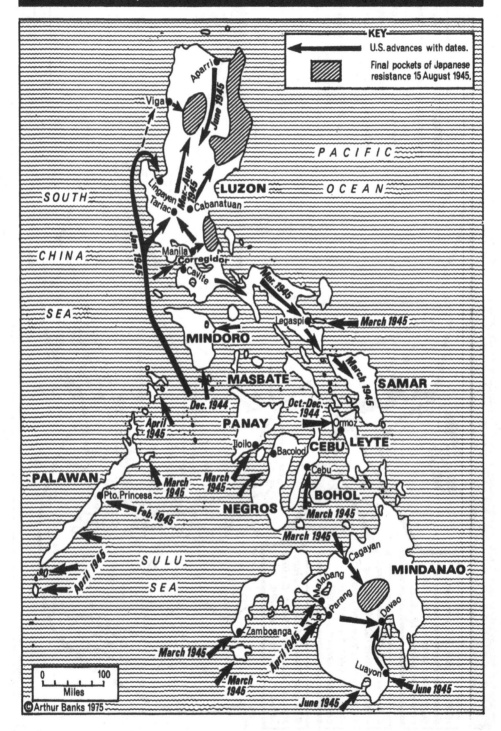

KEY
U.S. advances with dates.

Final pockets of Japanese resistance 15 August 1945.

PACIFIC OCEAN

Aparri

Viga

June 1945

SOUTH

Lingayen

Mar.-Aug. 1945

LUZON

Tarlac

Cabanatuan

CHINA

Jan. 1945

Manila

Corregidor

Cavite

SEA

Mar. 1945

MINDORO

Legaspi · March 1945

March 1945

MASBATE

SAMAR

Dec. 1944

Oct.-Dec. 1944

April 1945

PANAY

Ormoz

Iloilo

Bacolod

CEBU LEYTE

PALAWAN

March 1945

Cebu

BOHOL

Pto.Princesa

March 1945

NEGROS

March 1945

Feb. 1945

March 1945

March 1945

Cagayan

SULU

MINDANAO

SEA

Malabang

April 1945

Parang

Davao

Zamboanga

March 1945

April 1945

March 1945

Luayon

0   100

Miles

June 1945

June 1945

June 1945

© Arthur Banks 1975

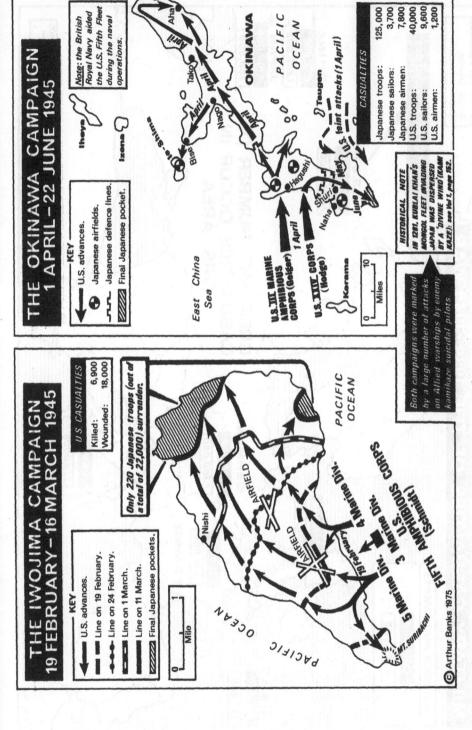

THE OKINAWA CAMPAIGN
1 APRIL – 22 JUNE 1945

Note: the British Royal Navy aided the U.S. Fifth Fleet during the naval operations.

KEY
U.S. advances.
Japanese airfields.
Japanese defence lines.
Final Japanese pocket.

OKINAWA

PACIFIC OCEAN

Iheya

Izena

Aha

Tako

Bise

Ie-Shima

Nago

Hagushi

Shuri

Naha

Nett

Teugen

U.S. feint attacks (1 April)

U.S. III MARINE AMPHIBIOUS CORPS (Geiger)

U.S. XXIV CORPS (Hodge)

1 April

June

Kerama

East China Sea

CASUALTIES

Japanese troops:	125,000
Japanese sailors:	3,700
Japanese airmen:	7,800
U.S. troops:	40,000
U.S. sailors:	9,600
U.S. airmen:	1,200

HISTORICAL NOTE
IN 1281, KUBLAI KHAN'S MONGOL FLEET INVADING JAPAN WAS DISPERSED BY A 'DIVINE WIND' (KAMIKAZE): see Vol 1, page 162.

0   10
Miles

Both campaigns were marked by a large number of attacks on Allied warships by enemy kamikaze suicidal pilots.

THE IWOJIMA CAMPAIGN
19 FEBRUARY – 16 MARCH 1945

U.S CASUALTIES
Killed: 6,900
Wounded: 18,000

Only 220 Japanese troops (out of a total of 22,000) surrender.

KEY
U.S. advances.
Line on 19 February.
Line on 24 February.
Line on 1 March.
Line on 11 March.
Final Japanese pockets.

PACIFIC OCEAN

PACIFIC OCEAN

Nishi

AIRFIELD

AIRFIELD

AIRFIELD

4 Marine Div.

3 Marine Div.

5 Marine Div.

19 February

MT. SURIBACHI

3 U.S. AMPHIBIOUS CORPS (Schmidt)

FIFTH AMPHIBIOUS (Schmidt)

0   1
Mile

© Arthur Banks 1975

MILITARY CASUALTIES OF THE 1939–1945 WAR

KEY
Deaths.
Wounded.

NOTE THESE HUGE CASUALTIES

U.S.S.R.
1,500,000
14,000,000

CHINA
650,000
7,800,000

JAPAN
1,510,000
500,000

ALL OTHER PARTICIPANTS
1,500,000
4,000,000

U.S.A.
293,000
590,000

BRITAIN
398,000
480,000

GERMANY
2,850,000
7,300,000

FRANCE
211,000
400,000

ITALY
78,000
120,000

GREATEST NUMBER OF
CASUALTIES OCCUR IN
THIS AREA

0   400
Miles

© Arthur Banks 1975

158

CIVIL CASUALTIES AND EXPENDITURE 1939–1945

KEY
Deaths.
Cost ($ millions).

JAPAN →
300,000
100,000

CHINA →
1,000,000
no figs. available

U.S.S.R.
15,000,000
200,000

NOTE THESE HIGH CIVILIAN CASUALTIES

Approximately 6,000,000 Jews in Germany and 4,500,000 Poles were killed (1939–1945).

POLAND

GERMANY
500,000
300,000

ITALY
80,000
50,000

BRITAIN
70,000
150,000

FRANCE
110,000
100,000

ALL OTHER PARTICIPANTS
15,000,000 ?
350,000

U.S.A. →
1,000 ?
350,000

NOTE THESE HIGH EXPENDITURES

0   400
Miles

© Arthur Banks 1975

159

THE WORLD'S SUPERPOWERS 1945

UNION OF SOVIET SOCIALIST REPUBLICS

Possessor of the largest army in the world and virtually self-sufficient in raw materials, however, due to German occupation, much of her industry is in ruins. She does not possess the over-riding weapon of all, the atomic bomb.

UNITED STATES OF AMERICA

Sole possessor of the atomic bomb makes her the world's leading military power: she possesses the largest air force and navy in the world. Furthermore, she is the world's leading industrial and manufacturing nation. Her homeland has remained inviolate throughout the war.

Britain, France, and Germany, the three European powers which had dominated the world scene prior to September 1939 emerged from the war much reduced in international status. From henceforth, the world's military spectrum was to be dominated by the U.S.A and the U.S.S.R., the two new superpowers.

PACIFIC OCEAN

INDIAN OCEAN

ATLANTIC OCEAN

AUSTRALIA

ANTARCTICA

ASIA

AFRICA

EUROPE

NORTH AMERICA

SOUTH AMERICA

Index of Place Names

Supplementary Index

Index of People